Neuro-Linguistic Programming

Read People And Think Positively And Successfully Using NLP to Kill Negativity, Procrastination, Fear And Phobias (Body Language, Positive Psychology, Productivity)

Adam Hunter

© Copyright 2018 - All rights reserved.

It is not legal to reproduce, duplicate, or transmit any part of this document in either electronic means or in printed format. Recording of this publication is strictly prohibited and any storage of this document is not allowed unless with written permission from the publisher except for the use of brief quotations in a book review.

Table Of Contents

Table Of Contents *3*
Introduction *1*
Chapter One: What is NLP? *5*
    Inception 5
    Expansion of the Development Team 6
    Books, Workshops, and More 8
    The Commercialization of NLP 9
    The Current State of NLP 9
    Uses of NLP 10
        Personal Life 10
        Professional Life 10
        Social Life 11

Chapter Two: Identify & Evaluate *13*
    Worry About the Future 13
    Worry About the Present 14
    Shame in Your Past 15

Chapter Three: The Power of the Subconscious Mind *17*

Chapter Four: NLP Training *23*
    Neuro 23
    Linguistic 24
    Programming 24
    Techniques 25
        Association – Music 25
        The Trigger 26

    Daily Affirmations 26
    Kill the Voices 27
    The Whiteout 27
    Grounding 28
    Take Words at Face Value 29
    Experimentation 30
    Anchoring 30
    Pacing 32
    The Pizza-Walk 32
    Mirroring 33
    The Swish 34

Chapter Five: NLP – Higher Level of Thinking 36

Using NLP for Yourself 36
    The Map isn't the Territory 37
    There is No Failure 37
    Communication and its Response 38
    You Cannot Fail to Communicate 38
    Dissociate Yourself 39
    Reframe 39
    Anchor Yourself 40
    Build Rapport 40
    Limiting Beliefs 40

Use NLP on Others 40
    The Antipodean Lilt 41
    Embedded Commands 41
    Restricting the Choice 42
    "I can, but I'd Rather Not" 43
    Know When to Use "and" and "but" 44
    Find out What People really Want 45

Chapter Six: Explaining VAK 47

Understanding Nonverbal Cues 48
    Facial Expressions 48
    Eye Contact 49
    Mouth 49
    Posture 49
    Touch 49

    Tone 50

Understanding Context 50
    The Conversation 51
    The Surrounding Area during the Conversation: 51
    Recent Experiences: 51
    Smile 52
    Eye Contact 52
    Jittery Movements... 52
    Posture 53
    Placement of Legs... 53
    Placement of Hands 53

Facial Expressions 54

Eyes 54
    Gazing 54
    Blinking 55
    Size of the Pupil 55

Mouth 55
    Pursed Lips 56
    Biting of the Lip 56
    Covering of the Mouth.. 56
    Gestures 56

Arms and Legs 57

Postures 57
    Open Posture 57
    Closed Posture 58

Personal Space 58
    Intimate Distance 58
    Personal Distance 58
    Social Distance 58

Chapter Seven: NLP and Anchoring 60

Steps to Create an Anchor 67
    Pick a Memory 67
    Association 67
    The Feeling 67

Release..68
Test 68
Repeat..68

Chapter Eight: NLP for Procrastination and Negative Beliefs Specifically..**69**

NLP for Procrastination.. **69**

NLP to Overcome Negative Beliefs 70

Dealing with Life...**74**

Making a Conscious Decision..**76**

Separate Your Thoughts **76**

Who is Thinking those Thoughts? **76**

Chapter Nine: NLP for Fear and Phobias **78**

Overcome Fear and Hesitation **78**

Overcome Phobias **83**
Avoid 83
Desensitization..83
Flooding 84

Chapter Ten: Other Ways to Support Positive Thinking **86**

Get Sufficient Sleep... **86**

Healthy Eating Habits **86**

Drink Plenty of Water **87**

Don't Forget to Treat Yourself **88**

Friends Matter.. **88**

Smile Often **89**

Enjoy Your Hobbies **89**

Stay Away from Negative People **90**

Don't Forget the Important Things in Life 90

Chapter Eleven: Maintaining Positivity 92

Overcome Obstacles 92
Focus on the Result 92
Define What You Want to Accomplish 92
Make a Note of the Reasons 92
If You Don't Do It 93
Setting Mini Goals 93
Scheduling 93
Marking Your Progress 93

Staying Consistent 94
Make a to-Do List 94
Create a Reward System 94
Breaking Up Your Workday 94
Don't Indulge in Any Activities that will Waste Your Time ... 94
Tackle the Tough Tasks First 95
Discuss Your Goals with Someone 95

Kill Procrastination 95
Figure Out the Reason 95
Getting Rid of the Obstacle 96
Just Get Started 96
Break it Down 96
The Right Environment 97
Rejoice in the Small Victories 97
Be Realistic 97
Self-Talk 98
Don't Try to be a Perfectionist 98

Chapter Twelve: Homework 99

One Problem per Day 99

Internalizing Intellectual Standards 100

Maintain an Intellectual Journal 100

Reshaping Your Character 101

Dealing with Your Egocentrism 101

Redefining the Way in which You See Things................102

Get in Touch with Your Emotions 102

Analyzing the Influence of a Group on Your Life..........103
- One Door Shuts and the Other Opens 103
- The Gift of Time 103
- Counting Kindness... 104
- The Funny Things 104
- Letter of Gratitude 104
- The Good Things 104
- Making Use of Your Signature Strengths 104

Conclusion... *105*

Resources *109*

Introduction

I thank you for choosing this book, Neuro-Linguistic Programming: Become the Person You Want to be Using NLP by Training your Brain to Think Positively to Create a Successful Life, and I hope you have a good time reading it.

In this age of cutthroat competition, it becomes all the more important that people utilize their mental capacity optimally to achieve success. Not doing so might leave you behind while your competitors surge forward. All human beings have the potential to multitask and can complete arduous tasks in no time. Not everyone is capable of doing this, and only those who realize their true mental potential, by training their mind to work at its optimal level, will be able to attain the success they dream of.

There will always be those who excel in their chosen field, and then there will be those who look up to them in envy. If everybody fell into the former category, then there would be no competition in this world; however, the main goal for a lot of us is to come out on top and leave the competition behind. So, what is it that differentiates the winners, and what do others lack? Well, the answer to this question lies in a simple concept: NLP.

Certain skills like self-confidence, good communication skills, and leadership abilities are important to be successful in all aspects of your life—personal as well as professional. For a lot of people, it is a necessity, and the lack of these qualities can make them feel inferior. Even if you possess all these skills, we can all use a good boost of self-confidence once in a while, but there is a small problem. The boost mentioned here is not available in the form of a tablet or a pill that you can purchase at your local drugstore. The only way to acquire it is by stepping out of your shell and summoning these qualities from within yourself. This is where NLP steps in.

NLP refers to neuro-linguistic programming, and it is a simple concept that allows a person to control their mind, and those of others, while influencing thoughts and behaviors to gain more out of life.

Well, why do you want to learn about NLP? Have you ever noticed that you are overcome with a wide range of negative emotions? Do you feel like your fears or your phobias control your life? Do you wonder where your negative emotions are sprouting from? Are you tired of looking at things through a vision that's tinted with negativity? Are you tired of all this, and do you want to change? If your answer is yes to all these questions or any one of them, then NLP can help you.

The world that we live in is overwrought with negative emotions. Negative emotions are those internal feelings that make us feel bad about ourselves and those around us. Negative emotions can be quite a hindrance when you want to achieve success in life. Well, here is a small secret about negative emotions: you can control them. Yes, you can control all that you feel, and you don't have to be a victim of your emotions. There are certain negative emotions that are generated in response to someone else. For instance, greed, envy, jealousy, or even hatred are often generated as a response to someone else's behavior. Do you ever find yourself feeling jealous of your colleague who seems to be doing well for himself even if you both do the same work? Negative emotions can also be a result of your internal feelings. For instance, your fears, doubt, lack of confidence, and such can also prevent you from achieving the success you want. Fears and phobias can prevent you from taking the action that you want to, and self-limiting beliefs can prevent you from excelling in your life.

If you want to correct any of these negative emotions, then this is the perfect book for you. The first step to fix a problem is to accept that you have a problem. Kudos to you—you understand the different aspects of life that you want to fix. The next step is to understand the primary cause of these issues. Once you understand that, the easy part is to fix them. It is quite easy to fix the way you think.

You need to understand that your brain is like any other muscle in your body. With a little training and conditioning, you can unleash your true potential. Most of us don't work at our maximum potential, and often there are certain things that prevent us from doing so. These reasons can be external as well as internal. It is a general misconception that you cannot control the way you think or feel. On the contrary, there are many things in life that you cannot control, but you can certainly control the way you think and feel. You cannot control the external events in life, but you can control your response to those events. The course of your life often depends on your responses to situations around you.

NLP is a technique that helps you reconfigure the way you think and process things. It is a very simple tool that helps you change the way you deal with your thoughts and emotions. At times, all that you need is a little perspective to change your life, and NLP will help you with that.

In this book, you will learn about the history of NLP; its benefits; its core concepts; ways in which you can use it in your daily life; tips to overcome limiting beliefs; steps to adopt a positive mindset and unleash the power of the subconscious mind; and other topics that will help you lead a successful life. If you want to help yourself to resolve these issues quickly and fulfill your goals easily, then this is the perfect book for you.

So, if you are ready, then let us start without further ado.

Chapter One: What is NLP?

In this chapter, you will learn about the origins and the history of neuro-linguistic programming.

Inception

Frank Pucelik, John Grinder, and Richard Bandler conducted studies on three therapists and this led to the inception of neuro-linguistic programming. They referred to it as a behavioral model at the time.

It all began when Richard Bandler met Frank Pucelik. Frank had returned from the Vietnam War and was quite traumatized by all that he had gone through. He found a friend in Richard Bandler. Bandler was a warehouse assistant at Bob Spitzer's publishing company, Science and Behavioral Books. As their friendship blossomed, Bandler and Pucelik decided to help each other rebuild their lives by copying the approaches mentioned in the transcripts and tapes of Bob Spitzer, most notably those of Fritz Perls (the founder of Gestalt Therapy). Initially, their only aim was to improve their own lives and they did not do it for any theoretical reasons.

The two of them started to practice Gestalt Therapy with a group at the University of California. After a while, they were joined by a young linguistics professor named John Grinder. He approached them with a couple of his observations and questions that marked the beginning of a long and successful relationship between these three that led to the birth of the modern-day topic of neuro-linguistic programming. When they started to work together, they began using their collective skills and creativity to analyze and model the works of other people like Fritz Perls and Virginia Satir, who is also known as the mother of family therapy. They studied the rate of success of these two therapists and wanted to emulate their studies by understanding the reasons for their success. They were introduced later on to Gregory Bateson, who introduced them to the works of Milton Erickson, a psychiatrist who specialized in medical hypnosis and family therapy.

Expansion of the Development Team

Once the ideas and insights started to flow, the core team was interested in trying them on others. This led to the expansion of the team as other friends joined them and helped them develop their work. Some of them were David Gordon, Robert Dilts, Judith DeLozier, and Leslie Cameron. There were many others who joined them subsequently and this highly creative group developed NLP.

Most of the methods that were developed during this phase are still a part of NLP training programs. Some of these techniques are anchoring, calibration, reframing, sensory acuity, and representational systems. A couple of other personal change methods, like the Change Personal History and New Behavioral Generator, are still practiced.

NLP and Tony Robbins

Business guru, Tony Robbins certainly seems to know it all. Tony Robbins achieved all the success that he did in his life with the help of NLP. In fact, NLP transformed his life. Robbins believes that knowledge isn't power, but it is merely a source of potential power.

Whenever you read something inspirational, have a rather brilliant idea or come across some life advice and tend to feel inspired and you vow to change your ways. The reality is quite different, isn't it? The inspiring moment passes you by, you don't do anything to follow through with it and it makes you feel frustrated. Therefore, it is not about what you know, but how you execute it that makes all the difference in life.

We are all usually conditioned to listen in a passive state. For instance, we might sit at the desk looking at the laptop, stretch out on the couch reading a book. Passive learning certainly doesn't inspire any action. Robbins recognized this pattern and decided to change it. He understood that the only way in which he can break this pattern is to use the information and act on it. The one thing that differentiates him from others is that he always follows through.

Robbins had a rough childhood and whatever he achieved in life, it was due to his determination and hard work. Success can mean different things to different people, but there is one equation that everyone can use to achieve the success that they want.

The first step is to understand your purpose.

Once you understand your purpose, you need to adopt the right mindset to stick to your goal. Robbins insists that you need to focus on the things that you want and not what you don't want, since energy follows focus. It is essentially the **law of attraction**.

Once you adopt a **positive mindset**, the next step is to take action. You need to consciously work towards your goal.

If you want to be successful, you need to work towards your goal and you also need to check your progress along the way. Assess your progress and proceed accordingly.

If you can change your approach towards how you deal with life and the problems you face, achieving success does become simpler.

These are the simple steps that Robbins followed which made him successful in life.

Books, Workshops, and More

The first publication on this subject was a two-volume book, *Structure of Magic I and II*. This book is considered to be one of the most difficult books to read about NLP because of its highly theoretical nature. During 1973-1976, when the group's creativity was at its peak, they developed new ideas and techniques, experimented with the concepts they already knew, conducted workshops, and wrote their first books, *The Structure of Magic I and II*. They also published *Patterns of Hypnotic Techniques of Milton H. Erickson, MD, Volume 1* in 1975, focusing on Erickson's use of language, their initial model. Apart from this, they also released *Erickson* Volume 2 in 1977.

John O. Stevens transcribed and edited the tapes from their earlier workshops and published them under the title *Frogs into Princes* in 1979. Just like most books on NLP at that time, the book also focused on therapists who wanted to help their patients. These books challenged the traditional way of thinking and offered practical alternatives. These books successfully convinced several therapists to try NLP. Bandler and Grinder continue to organize workshops about NLP throughout the seventies and, towards the late seventies, they had become so popular that their workshops were always packed.

The Commercialization of NLP

The creativity and excitement about NLP inspired a lot of people during the seventies, but this excitement was quickly overshadowed in the eighties. People started to care more about commercial issues, and there was a lot of debate about who was doing it right and who owned it. During this time, Grinder and Bandler parted ways and there is said to be some bitterness between them. They worked on developing their own ideas of NLP from that point on and soon NLP became a way to gain power over one's life as well as that of others. It was no longer a simple route to self-discovery but was considered to be a product that could be marketed to people who wanted quick results.

The Current State of NLP

At present, there is no one particular type of NLP. After Bandler and Grinder parted ways, different NLP camps emerged. The two obvious camps consisted of supporters of Grinder and Bandler, but that was just the beginning. Soon, there were Tony Robbins camps and Lesley Cameron-Bandler camps and many others followed suit. NLP was coming of age and all this diversity reflected its growth.

NLP is more of a movement than an ideology these days. It refers to a body of ideas and knowledge that are constantly developing and diversifying. It is a wonderful and creative concept and one person cannot claim ownership of it. NLP is a personal concept that everyone individualizes to suit their needs.

Uses of NLP

You can use NLP in your personal and professional life.

Personal Life

Communication helps you express your feelings and is an extremely important aspect of any relationship. You can learn to avoid unnecessary fights or misunderstandings so that you have some peace of mind. Not just that, positive communication will bring you closer together as a family and will help you lead a better life.

NLP will teach you to value yourself. Perception of yourself plays a critical role in how you respond to things. Usually, people tend to be a little hard on themselves.

If you want success, then you need to love and accept yourself. You need to accept your thought process and learn to evaluate it as well. You must not beat yourself up for the negative aspects and must instead work to change them.

NLP will bring about an overall change that is quite positive. It will help create an ideal relationship between you and your family members that is devoid of all unnecessary tensions. The rapport that you share with those you love will help strengthen your self-confidence.

Professional Life

Professionally, you can attain a lot of benefits by implementing NLP. For starters, it is a good technique that you can use for solving problems. One of the most important tasks that you will be faced with in any professional setting is solving problems. In fact, if you can effectively solve problems, it is your chance to shine and get noticed. You might be able to impress your boss and even get a promotion. To do this, you need to know how to use NLP to solve problems effectively. Communication is critical, and you need to communicate effectively with your colleagues and coworkers, listening to their feedback before you can decide on a solution.

With NLP, you will be able to easily manage different people in your office. Personnel management can be cumbersome, but it is an important aspect of your professional life. If you want to be successful at work, then you need to be able to successfully manage people and make sure that everyone is on the same page. NLP will teach you to be patient and lead the way. You will find it rather easy not just listen to everyone, but to make others listen to you as well.

Leadership skills are important, especially if you wish to see yourself progress. NLP will teach you the necessary leadership skills to move ahead in life. You will be able to take the right action at the right time and make others follow it as well. Apart from this, your ability to communicate effectively with others and your team will help you become invincible at work. Once you program your brain to work efficiently and remove all obstacles, then you will be able to achieve your targets rather easily.

Social Life

You can use NLP in your social life as well. NLP helps with networking. Once you know how to read someone else's body language, verbal cues, and nonverbal cues, you can communicate effectively. Effective communication is the easiest way to network with others. NLP will help you make new friends and also hold onto the ones you already have.

NLP will help you increase your social responsibility. As you know, it is important for you to give back to society. You can contribute in any which way you like as long as you think it will help you establish a positive impact. Again, it is not limited to just these benefits. You will learn about the many other uses of NLP.

Chapter Two: Identify & Evaluate

Everyone has negative and positive thoughts throughout the day. The positivity quotient in your life depends on the way you deal with the negative thoughts. You can ignore such thoughts, accept them as truth, or confront them. These negative thoughts can weigh you down and suck the life out of you.

In this section, you will learn about the different reasons for all the negative thoughts that you think.

Worry About the Future

Everyone is scared of the unknown, and since you cannot predict your future, a common fear is the fear of the future. People have been continually trying to predict future since the beginning of time. They have tried different things like looking at cracked turtle shells, observing the way birds fly, and the different constellations and positions of stars in the sky. People tend to be scared of the future and all that it might bring.

Will your future bring you fortune or misery? With the advancement of science, people can successfully predict certain short-term outcomes within a closed system like the weather or the elections; however, the average person spends a lot of his or her time worrying about what might or might not happen in the near or distant future.

A lot of people try to maintain a positive outlook about the future and think that they will succeed or achieve the goals that they have set for themselves if they keep trying and don't give up. Well, that's one set of the population that manages to keep a positive outlook, but the rest worry about the future, and the fear of failure is quite real. We all tend to waste a lot of our time and energy thinking about scenarios that might or might not happen. A simple analogy will help put things in perspective for you. The way we worry about the future is similar to paying interest on a credit card that you have yet to use.

You need to understand that the future doesn't exist yet. The fear of the future stems from the fact that we don't have any control over it. One of the easiest ways in which you can regain some control in your life is to plan for the future. You can create a step-by-step plan for yourself. No plan can help you predict the future, but a plan of action can help you regain some control over your life. You can make short-term as well as long-term plans for yourself. A plan will help reduce the fear of future and it will, in turn, reduce any negative thoughts that you have about the future.

Worry About the Present

It isn't just the future that we worry about; we worry about the present too. We worry about the things that are happening or aren't happening in our lives. Worry is a mere extension of fear, and this fear can have a crippling effect on your life. For instance, you might worry about what your kids are doing at school, your finances, or even your work. You may worry about something as simple as whether you locked the car door or not. Phew, that's a lot of worries that we carry.

Imagine how productive your day would be if you didn't worry so much. Well, the good news is that there is a simple way in which you can combat all this fear that you experience. All that you need to do is create a daily schedule for yourself. When you have a schedule to follow, then you can increase your productivity and concentrate on all those things that are important.

Shame in Your Past

We all tend to do things that we aren't proud of. In fact, we might do various things that we find embarrassing. We all make mistakes, and some of those mistakes can haunt us in our present. Well, you cannot let your past control your life. You need to understand that your past is a part of your life and you cannot do anything to change your past. All that you can do is learn from your mistakes and prevent them from happening again. Think of your past as a valuable lesson and nothing else. Your past does not define you. All that you do in your present will shape your future, but your past has no role to play in your present. Instead of worrying about every mistake you have ever made, think about the ways in which you can fix them and learn from them. It is time to regain control of your life and live in the present. If you live in the past or the future, and all that you do is worry about them, you will end up with a list of self-limiting beliefs that will prevent you from attaining any form of success in your life.

You need to understand that your thoughts shape your life. You can control your life and, in fact, you are the only one that can control your thoughts. If you think positive thoughts, you will feel good about yourself, those around you, and life in general; however, negative thoughts can make you feel bad and can disrupt your productivity. Imagine how productive your life would be if you didn't spend your time worrying about negative thoughts.

The easiest way to deal with negative thoughts is to understand their root cause and replace them with positive messages. For instance, if you feel stuck, or if you face an impossibly difficult obstacle, then instead of thinking that you must give up because you cannot deal with it, you can replace this negative thought with a positive one like "maybe I need to change the way I am looking at the problem and try a different approach."

Your thoughts have the power to control and change your life. Therefore, it is important that you make sure that you are in control of them and not the other way around. You cannot get anything done in life if you allow negativity to hold you back.

Chapter Three: The Power of the Subconscious Mind

When you are learning how to drive a car, in the initial stages you tend to be really focused and alert. Your mind will be fully involved in the task at hand, which is driving. After a while, when you have mastered the skill, then you will notice that you needn't be 100 percent focused on driving. Instead, you can listen to music or even talk to others while you are driving your car, without losing control of the vehicle. So, what does this mean, and what part of your mind is controlling the activity you perform? Has this activity been delegated to some other part without your conscious knowledge?

If an object comes near your eyes, then even before you are aware of what exactly has happened, you will blink. How did your body generate this reaction? When you accidentally touch a naked electrical wire or anything hot, what's that mysterious force that is responsible for you pulling back your hand immediately, before you have even managed to figure out what's going on? Why is it easier to change some of your behaviors and habits, even though you want to consciously change all of them? Who or what is responsible for this? Who oversees all these actions and reactions?

The mind is made up of two parts—the conscious and the unconscious mind. Understanding the difference between these two forms the crux of trying to understand human behavior. When you are performing a task and are aware of what you are doing, then such an action will be the action performed by your conscious mind.

Human beings tend to have a very limited attention span. The conscious mind is responsible for learning the task that is required to be performed repeatedly, and then it hands over the reins to the subconscious mind so that the conscious mind will be free to learn other tasks or concentrate on things that require immediate attention. For instance, when you are brushing your teeth, your conscious mind can drift away, and you might start remembering the things that you did all day long or think about the things that you haven't done yet. When this happens, your subconscious mind takes over the activity of brushing your teeth. Any activity that is dull, repetitive, and habitual, like brushing your teeth, will be unworthy of your conscious mind and its attention can be instead focused on thinking about more important functions that need to be performed.

The conscious mind functions as a filter and a logical processor of the information that you receive from the external environment. Based on this information that you receive, your beliefs are formed and then stored in your subconscious mind so that your behavior that is consistent with such beliefs is being carried on its own.

If someone asks you what two plus two is then you will use your conscious mind to answer the question. Similarly, when someone tells you that the earth is flat, then this information will be processed by your conscious mind and interpreted by it, only to find the answer that the earth is spherical and therefore your conscious mind will reject that information, filtering it before it turns into a belief.

If you think of your conscious mind as a filter, then your subconscious mind is the recorder. It is subtler, and the psychology of an individual revolves almost entirely around it. You might have some idea regarding situations in which your subconscious mind comes to the forefront. As mentioned earlier, when you touch something hot, before you even realize it, you will pull your hand back within the blink of an eye. It is a reflex action and is governed by the subconscious mind. The conscious mind always requires some time for processing and therefore is comparatively slower. The subconscious mind is fast and automatic in nature.

The subconscious mind can be perceived as a video recorder that absorbs all the information that you have been exposed to so far. It includes all your experiences, skills acquired, and also your evolutionary history! All this information is too much for your conscious mind to hold; given that it must constantly deal with the present moment, it will be necessary to create a storage system for holding onto all the information that you have acquired. Your subconscious mind is this storage unit.

The human brain tends to work on thought patterns that are nothing but programs that have been embedded into the neural network. You might observe that there is a definite pattern to some of the thoughts that have been produced by your brain. For instance, your brain might be currently involved in the habit of creating a negative pattern of thinking and it will lend a negative flavor to all the information that is being interpreted by it. In such a case, your subconscious mind is looking at reality through the lens of negativity and the root of all this negativity will be a subconscious belief present in some so-called "core" negative thoughts.

The main problem with such subconscious patterns is that you tend to take them for what they seem to be and start believing that they're the absolute truth. However, the truth is simply that the subconscious patterns are the thought patterns that have been through your mind so many times that they have attained an automatic mode of functioning. You can rid yourself of all this negativity in your subconscious mind by not paying any attention to them.

All the thoughts that are running on "automatic" mode form your subconscious mind. All these subconscious thoughts can be observed when the awareness of your mind has been deepened and you can observe the way these core thoughts are essential to most of our perceptions and interpretations. The only obstacle is that, because most of these subconscious thoughts are running automatically, you might presume that they are true and make them a part of your identity. You need to remember that all these core thoughts embedded into your subconscious were all "new" thoughts at one point in time. Some of negative subconscious thoughts are "I will always remain fat, irrespective of what I do"; "I cannot trust anyone"; "I am not good looking"; "and I am not smart enough to make money," and so on. You might have similar negative thoughts at one point of time in your life or another and these thoughts are now running on automatic mode. These core negative thoughts color your perception of reality with negativity.

You need to understand that there is no truth to any of this negativity. Negative thinking only helps foster more negativity and it stops you from moving towards well-being in life. You need to let your awareness deepen and start seeing through all the negativity that exists in your subconscious. It is the only way in which you can get rid yourself of all the negative patterns that you have come to believe in.

Your subconscious is responsible for managing the energies of your heart and it takes this job very seriously. The subconscious mind speaks in a language that consists of physiological feelings and emotions that can be transmitted throughout your body.

The primary directive of your subconscious is your survival. When it thinks that you are incapable of handling disappointment, fear, or any other negative emotion, it immediately takes over. The first reason why you must influence your subconscious is that it helps in providing the much-needed assurance that you can handle feeling vulnerable without being overwhelmed by it. If your perceptions tell you that you cannot, then your subconscious automatically shifts into protective mode. Its secondary directive is to make sure that you thrive. You are designed in a way to not merely survive but so that you are driven by an inner force that motivates you to thrive. You are designed in an exquisite manner to serve a twofold purpose of connecting in a way that's meaningful and also of being your true self while you are in the process of relating to others and life alike. The subconscious shapes your behavior. If you want to thrive, you need to know how to calm yourself and to assure yourself when your fear of survival surfaces, like feelings of rejection, abandonment, or even inadequacy. If you don't feel safe enough to love somebody, then your body will automatically go into "automatic" mode to protect itself.

Infinite riches are present all around you; you just have to open your mental eyes to be able to see for yourself the treasure chest of infinity that is hidden within you. Everything that you need to live a glorious life is within you; you just need to tap into this hidden resource. There are different ways in which you can awaken the power of your subconscious mind. You can access your subconscious by visualization, meditation, dreaming, and so on. In the coming chapters, you will learn about the different NLP techniques that you can use to reprogram your subconscious.

Chapter Four: NLP Training

NLP stands for neuro-linguistic programming, and these are the three core concepts that you need to learn about.

Neuro

Neuro stands for anything that is related to the brain. You have probably come across the concept of neurology at some point. Neurology refers to the study of the brain. On any given day, all our senses work together to help us pick up different stimuli from our surroundings. It can be the odors you smell, the sounds you hear, textures you feel, or even the sights you see. All the senses pick up these stimuli and relay them to your brain; your brain then generates an apt response. The human mind consists of two parts—the conscious mind and the subconscious mind. The conscious mind helps you make all decisions and governs your senses. The subconscious mind is more like an autopilot mode where you don't need to instruct your brain. Even if your subconscious mind helps you perform certain tasks automatically, you still need to consult your conscious mind daily.

What if you can reduce some of that load on your conscious mind? What if you can empower your subconscious mind to make a lot of your decisions? It will certainly make your life easy, won't it? NLP helps your conscious mind converge with your subconscious mind.

Your mind will be able to relate and respond faster to things that are similar in nature. It will be like collecting all the information that lies in your brain and sending it to specific folders that will keep the information safe for a long time. You need to simply extrapolate the information and apply it to the different situations that arise in your life.

Linguistic

The next core concept of NLP is linguistics. Linguistics refers to the study of languages. You cannot communicate effectively if your language skills aren't adequate. If others cannot understand what you are saying, or if you don't understand what they are telling you, then how can you progress? Language barriers can be annoying, especially if they are internal in nature. Human beings are amongst the most expressive creatures on earth and it is quite a shame if we are unable to effectively express our thoughts and feelings. If you want to get your point across, then you need to improve the way you speak. You need to put some effort into establishing better communication skills. At the same time, you need to be good at internal communication as well. Internal communication is critical, and you need to be able to express yourself quickly so that you can take immediate action. If your mind tells you one thing and you do something else, then things will never work in your favor. You need to be able to think clearly and express yourself clearly as well.

Programming

The third concept is the programming. Programming refers to the bifurcation of information and the process of sending such information to different folders in your brain. You need to program yourself in a manner that is conducive to productivity and which helps you make the most of your skillset. When we are young, our minds are fresh, impressionable, and can capture a lot of information. Not just that, but we can also remember things for longer. However, with age, this aspect of our mind starts to change, and it starts to become difficult to process and store information. You can fix this problem with NLP. NLP will help you not just acquire information, but also divide and store it in a simple manner in your memory. Once you understand these core concepts, you can learn about the techniques of NLP. You need to understand that your brain is like any other muscle in your body and you can train it. You can train yourself to be goal-oriented and your mind will not rest until you achieve your goals.

Techniques

Association – Music

For a lot of people, music is an important part of their life. The genre of music doesn't matter; it can be anything that you enjoy. Music tends to have a sway over us that not many things do. It can also influence the way a person feels. It is one of the reasons why music therapy is quite popular. Music helps with our feelings. This is the reason why it is a technique of association included in NLP.

This exercise is about linking a particular song with a feeling of confidence and boosting your self-esteem in this manner. Different people tend to have different feelings about a song; you probably have a song that makes you feel like you are on top of the world. Take a couple of minutes and go through your playlist and find a song that makes you feel confident or inspired. Once you choose a song, you simply need to hum it or sing it whenever you feel down. If you want, you can always pretend to play an imaginary guitar to feel better.

The Trigger

This is a visualization exercise. You need to find a quiet and comfortable spot for this exercise. Now, sit down and close your eyes. Make sure that your breathing is regular, and calm your mind. When you feel calm, open your eyes and try to visualize a mirror image of yourself in front of you. The image that you visualize is self-assured, successful, and reacts differently to things. Focus on this image and study how it behaves.

After you have analyzed this image thoroughly, it is time to put yourself in its shoes. Feel its strength coursing through your body and feel just as confident as that image. This is going to be your trigger from now on. Whenever you want to feel powerful again, repeat this exercise again. The more you practice, the stronger it will become.

Daily Affirmations

Start your day with some daily affirmations. It is the best way to make sure you start your day on a positive note and ensure that you don't miss the opportunity to feel confident daily. You need to make some time for yourself in the morning and think about all the good things about yourself. You must remember that you are the only one that has the power to do what you want, and you have the key to make yourself feel good about yourself. If you want to achieve something, then instead of telling yourself that you will get there, you need to feel like you are already there. Feel like you are the person that you want to be and have achieved the things that you want to.

Kill the Voices

We all experience moments of weakness, where a nagging voice inside our heads tells us that we aren't good enough. It keeps reminding us that someone doesn't like us or that we haven't achieved anything yet. This little voice is really good at spouting destructive thoughts that can remove all traces of motivation that we might have.

Now try to think of the last time you heard this nagging voice in your head. Do you recognize this voice? Is it yours or someone else's? When you have a clear idea of whose voice it is, it is time to change the voice.

This exercise is pretty simple and helps kill that nagging voice in your head. Think of different scenarios and put the voice in such scenarios to render it ineffective. Think of how the voice would sound if it belonged to Donald Duck or any other Disney character. Try to imagine a funny scene where the speaker of the voice is trying to sound serious but cannot pull it off. It will help reduce the effect the nagging voice has on you. It is quite like the manner in which the wizards in Harry Potter defeat a Boggart. The Boggart can materialize their worst fear, and when they imagine it in a funny context, the Boggart loses all its power.

The Whiteout

We all have memories that can surface at inappropriate times, make us feel uncomfortable, and prevent us from giving our best.

We have memories that can surface at the most inappropriate times and make us feel uncomfortable, therefore inhibiting us from giving our best. They are deeply rooted in our subconscious because we have had a bad experience associated with them. The whiteout technique aims at enabling you to stop thinking about such memories at will.

First of all, think of a memory that makes you feel uncomfortable. It can be about a time you embarrassed yourself or when you performed exceptionally badly at something. Once you have the image established clearly in your mind, literally turn up the brightness of the image quickly. Do it very fast, so that the image goes absolutely white.

After this, pause for a second and think of something entirely different.. Repeat the process in quick succession at least six or seven times, and then pause to see what happens. When you will think of the uncomfortable memory again, either it will whiteout all by itself, or you won't be able to see it clearly. Adding a sound effect to the whiteout process can help.

Make sure to pause between each cycle so that your brain doesn't create a loop of the image and the whiteout.

Grounding

This is another basic NLP technique which is really important to learn before you work on some other advanced techniques. It helps you get your confidence issues sorted out and develop a solid foundation from which to work upwards. For this technique, you must be barefoot, but if you can't do that, make sure you are not wearing high heels.

Stand up straight and keep your feet shoulder-width apart and completely flat on the ground. Then move your hips forward slightly and feel your stomach muscles going slightly tense. Your shoulders and arms will be a little loose and your thighs will tense up slightly. Now slightly unlock your knees but don't bend them, and take deep, long breaths, keeping your eyes focused ahead of you. Focus your attention on a point a couple of centimeters below the navel and notice how you feel.

Practice this posture a few times every day, and once you are comfortable with it, try moving around in it. Make sure you are breathing correctly as you move around, and maintain the posture. It will start feeling natural in a while and will help you stay mentally and physically grounded in the reality around you.

Take Words at Face Value

One of the secrets of getting really good at NLP is to take what people say quite literally. It can seem really absurd to some people. After all, we don't always exactly mean what we say. Some things are said just for dramatic value, while others are intended to stress something.

But if you really want to understand the psychology of someone you are talking to, you have to take them literally. People will tell you all you need to know in just the first couple of minutes. You just have to exhibit openness and ask the right questions. For example, if someone tells you they just can't envision themselves losing weight, you must not try to convince them that they can. Instead, you can try and make them see things from a different perspective.

See, people don't like to "lose" things. If that is what you set as a goal, you are bound to fail in most cases. People also don't process negatives as well as they process positives. So telling someone not to think about an elephant will result in just the opposite. It is all wired into our neurology.

Experimentation

The way our communication works is deeply set into our subconscious. When we talk, we subconsciously have a goal in mind, whether we are aware of it or not, and all of our communication is aimed at fulfilling that goal, even if we don't consciously frame our responses.

Try to remember your last leisurely telephone conversation. You will notice that you were not paying much attention to the conversation at least half the time. Your mind was still forming coherent thoughts that manifested into proper replies. This is because language, vocabulary, and grammar are deeply embedded in your subconscious mind.

To become good at communication, you have to experiment with this. Think of yourself as a baby who is still learning and has no concept of failure. Try different phrases and words as you interact with someone you trust, maybe a fellow NLP-practicing buddy. Notice how you get better with time.

Anchoring

A really useful NLP technique for inducing a certain mental state or emotion is anchoring. It can help you enter a mental frame of happiness, relaxation, focus, or anything else you desire, at will. This technique usually requires a touch, gesture, or verbal cue to be used as an "anchor." This anchor acts as a bookmark for you to recall an emotion or state of mind at will whenever you want to.

To understand how the process of anchoring works, let's take a look at an example. For this, first of all, you need to think about a time when you felt really happy. Try to remember one such memory. It can be a time when you won a race that meant a lot to you, or when you had a baby, or maybe when you had your first kiss. Anything you consider a really happy moment will do. Now try to think of the moments before that moment. What happened before the happy moment? Try to create a story leading to that particular moment, and picture it in your head, recalling everything you felt at that time. Try to be as vivid as possible.

When you are at the pinnacle of such feelings, take the index finger and middle finger on your left hand, and place them in your right hand. Then give two gentle but quick squeezes to the fingers. When you squeeze them for the second time, try to picture the happy moment in a larger frame, as if it were closer to you than before. Imagine the feeling growing exponentially and getting stronger inside you.

After this, it is only a game of repetition. Try to describe the feeling again, recalling exactly what you felt at that moment. Then squeeze the same two fingers with your right hand again, and make the picture larger during the second squeeze. After a while of doing this, you will notice that the happy feeling doubles all by itself, without you having to force it to grow. Your progress with this technique will become even faster if you can imagine the feeling really clearly and remember the moment very vividly. Repeat this process at least five times and you will start to feel the effects soon.

Now you have laid the anchor. When you have become adept at this technique, it will become extremely easy for you to recall this anchor at any time by squeezing your fingers twice. You will feel happy instantly just by recalling the anchor.

Pacing

Pacing is a technique that you can use to influence others. When you use this technique, you can enter the other person's model of reality on their terms. It is quite similar to walking next to someone at their own pace. Once you have paced them, and have managed to establish a rapport and have displayed that you understand them, the next thing you need to do is lead them. You essentially use the rapport that you have built from pacing to influence someone else.

For instance, if you want to convince someone to act in a particular manner, the first thing that you need to do is understand why they act in the manner that they do. Once you try to understand this, you can then work on establishing a rapport with them. You need to find some common ground and use that to understand the other person. Once the other person realizes that you both think alike, they will automatically become more receptive to your suggestions.

The Pizza-Walk

From early on, we are taught to think of mistakes as dangerous. It is part of our social conditioning. And for this reason, our nervous system protects us from dangerous situations. What we must understand is that making mistakes is an extremely important part of learning. If you want to be skilled at NLP, you have to give yourself the chance to fail.

A problem many people face when they want to do something is hesitation. To remove hesitation, I like to suggest a method called the Pizza-Walk Experience. It costs almost nothing and can be done anywhere. This exercise will help you let go of all the unnecessary hesitation that holds you back from doing your best.

Think about some of the areas in your life in which you hesitate. After this, go to any commercial space of your choice, like a restaurant or a gas station, and ask for something completely absurd which you are sure you won't find there. Keep a straight face when you request it, and be polite and non-threatening. Repeat this process at least twice in the following week. Notice the change in your responses in situations where you might have hesitated in the past.

It is really that simple. Hesitation is one of the greatest barriers to learning, and with this technique you can completely remove unwanted hesitation in any part of your life. You want to ask out a girl you really like but are hesitating? You want to apply for the new job in a local tech company but are not sure if you are good enough? Go for the pizza-walk and then see the change.

Mirroring

Mirroring is a simple technique that essentially implies that you need to copy another person. Like the name suggests, in mirroring, you need to copy another person's gestures, tone of the voice, movements or even certain catchphrases.

All humans are hard-wired to like and feel comfortable around other humans. In fact, this is an evolutionary advantage. The closer we live together, the higher are our chances of survival as a species. So, anything that is not similar to you will make you feel uncomfortable. You will feel comfortable only around those with whom you feel like you share some similarity. Mirroring uses this concept.

In mirroring, you need to essentially convince the other person that you are similar to them. It is a simple technique that you can use to influence others. The next time you are around someone you like or feel comfortable with, you will notice that you have adopted certain similar gestures that are mirror images of each other. You don't do this consciously, but it is your subconscious that guides you. When you try to mirror someone during a conversation, then make sure that you don't abruptly start mirroring their gestures. You need to do this slowly and gradually because you are trying to influence their subconscious mind.

Start to slowly copy their gestures until your gestures look like a mirror image of theirs. If they change a specific gesture, you can slowly change yours too. If you want to make sure that mirroring works for you, once you know that someone is comfortable with you, you need to try a new gesture. If the other person unconsciously copies your gesture, then it works!

The Swish

The Swish is a rather advanced NLP technique. It doesn't make you forget a bad memory or a negative feeling, but it helps point you in a new direction altogether. You know about the anchoring technique and how you can create anchors to recall certain positive feelings; however, at times, our brain can unknowingly also create negative anchors. When your brain creates negative anchors, then it can trigger unwanted feelings at unfortunate times. The Swish technique helps recode and even delete such negative anchors.

In this exercise, think of an unwanted feeling and image or an associated memory that triggers such a feeling. You need to remove that particular image before the bad feeling sets in. This is the trigger, and you need to replace it with a good feeling and trigger. Place this image such that it is superimposed upon the negative one. You only need speed and not accuracy. Then open your eyes and return to reality. Repeat this at least five times and try to make the Swish quicker each time. After a couple of days, test it to see whether the negative image comes back or not. If it does, then you need to replace it with a powerful image or memory that is more potent.

Chapter Five: NLP – Higher Level of Thinking

Using NLP for Yourself

There are different ways in which you can describe NLP, and this is one of the reasons why it is difficult to find a clear definition of NLP. Also, the name seems pretty vague, doesn't it? Richard Bandler, in one of his workshops, recalled an anecdote on how he came up with the name. Apparently, on one fine day when he was driving, he placed a couple of books about neurology, linguistics, and computer programming on the passenger seat. The police stopped him for speeding. As justification, he tried to explain to the policeman that he was speeding because he was late for a conference. The policeman found this reason dubious and asked him what the conference was about. So, Bandler being the quick thinker that he was, looked over at the passenger seat and replied that the conference was about neuro-linguistic programming. Apparently this is how he came up with the name of NLP. Well, this story might or might not be accurate. In this section, you will learn more about an important aspect of NLP, and that is the mindset.

Even though NLP includes various techniques to change the way you think, the most important concept in NLP is about the mindset.

So, how can you define the term mindset? The best way to describe mindset is as NLP presuppositions. Mindset refers to the assumptions or the principles that a person chooses to adopt in daily life. It is a person's way of looking at the world. The mindset is much more powerful than the simple NLP techniques. In this section, you will learn about using NLP on yourself and others. You can use NLP to influence your mindset so that you feel powerful and in control of your life.

The Map isn't the Territory

It means that our perception of reality is merely a perception and not reality. We often tend to jump to the conclusion that what happens around us is true even when it is often only our interpretation of what we think happened. The difficulty crops up because we seem to react to such events as if they are true. There is a presupposition in NLP that, often, people respond to an experience and not to reality. So, this presupposition reminds you that you need to question what you believe and see if you might have unknowingly distorted it. For instance, if you have an argument with your loved one, in the course of the argument certain heated words are bound to be exchanged. After such an argument, do you start to believe the harsh words your loved one said? You might even hold onto those words and start feeling terrible about yourself. The reality is that your loved one probably didn't mean what was said and you have probably taken it out of context. So, your memory of the reality you think happened, and the reality itself, are quite different.

There is No Failure

Will you feel different if every time you don't achieve your goal, you see that as an opportunity to learn and not a failure? The general conditioning in society is such that if a person doesn't achieve a goal, he or she is deemed to be a failure. Will you start beating yourself about it and start to judge yourself harshly for failing? How about you try to replace this negative thinking with something more neutral and positive? What if every time you don't achieve something, you merely think of it as an opportunity to learn and to do better? A little positive communication with yourself can change the way you view yourself and the world around you.

Communication and its Response

The meaning of communication is the response or the reaction you receive. This one might sound quite tricky. Most of the time, we think that we are being quite clear in the way we communicate, and it seems like our intention isn't being understood or that the message isn't coming across as we intended. It is certainly easier to blame the receiver for the miscommunication; however, it will do you some good if you accept some responsibility in all this. Yes, you were probably clear in what you said, and the other person didn't understand you, but does it matter? If the message doesn't get through, it doesn't matter who is at fault! Isn't it simpler to focus on the best means to get the communication going? This is where NLP comes into the picture. NLP suggests that, the more flexible the communication, the higher the rate of success. There is a presupposition in NLP that, in any system, the element that has the most flexibility will exert the most influence. Therefore, if you are a little flexible in the way you communicate, the chances of you being misunderstood are quite low.

You Cannot Fail to Communicate

Regardless of what you do or don't say, or what you do or don't do, you are still communicating. Even when you are silent and don't express your opinion, you are communicating. Verbal communication isn't the only way to communicate, and nonverbal communication is as important as verbal communication. Your body language, expressions, the tone of your voice, and such are important aspects of communication. You will learn about all this in the next chapter.

You need to learn to establish some positive communication with yourself. If you can influence your mind to think positive thoughts, then your perception of yourself and your life will be positive. You need to let go of any negative beliefs you have and replace them with all things positive.

There are five ways in which you can use NLP to transform yourself for the better.

Dissociate Yourself

Emotional stress can consume you. If you leave it unaddressed, then all the negative emotions can prevent you from evolving and succeeding in life. NLP can help neutralize such feelings and will help you view a situation rationally. When you can view something rationally, or when you can rationalize something, the way you react and respond to it will differ. Instead of letting your anger, worries, or stress get the better of you, you need to learn to dissociate yourself from all that negativity.

Reframe

There will always be situations that will make you feel powerless and when you will be overcome by emotions. In such situations, you need to reframe the content so that you can focus on the things that are important and reduce your stress. You need to remember that there are positive and negative aspects of any situation. If you can merely change the way you view something, then you can shift your focus from all the things that don't matter and can instead concentrate on the things that do matter.

Anchor Yourself

If you want to work on positive emotional responses, even in stressful situations, then anchoring will help you. By consciously channeling a positive state of mind, you will be able to alter the way you feel in any given situation.

Build Rapport

Life is all about establishing communication and building relationships. With the help of NLP, you can build rapport with anyone in your personal and professional life. You will learn to connect with a person through their body language and their communication as well as their breathing patterns. Once you learn to pay attention to the other person, you can easily mirror the way they behave, and it will help you build a rapport.

Limiting Beliefs

The only thing that stops a person from being successful is his or her limiting beliefs. You need to learn to identify limiting beliefs that you might have, and you need to correct them. You cannot simply ignore your limiting beliefs because they can have a crippling effect on your psyche. You are the only one that can change the way you think about yourself. The different NLP techniques discussed in the previous chapter will help you change any limiting beliefs you have about yourself.

Use NLP on Others

People want different things out of NLP, but one common theme among the various expectations people have from NLP is the ability to be able to persuade people better. In this section, you will learn about the different techniques of NLP that you can use to persuade or influence others.

The Antipodean Lilt

First things first, let's talk about the antipodean lilt for a bit. You may have heard of it already, as it is a very popular concept. It's not very potent. It can help you deal better with children, but it doesn't work great for persuasion.

If you don't know what it is, let me explain it in brief. It happens when you let your voice rise in pitch at the end of a sentence. For example, if you say, "I'm going back to Sydney" in a way that the last bit rises up and sounds like a question, it makes you seem unsure. On the other hand, if you say the same part with a lower voice, it sounds more confident and commanding. As a result, the listener feels more confident in what you're about to do, too.

This is a very basic technique that probably won't work on a lot of people, but it still helps to know it.

Embedded Commands

So let's talk about embedded commands. This is one of the simpler yet more powerful techniques. In this technique, you make use of an embedded command in your sentence without being impolite. This makes it difficult for the other person to say no.

Let me give you an example. If you go out often to drink with your friends, think back to one of the times when you were sitting together having drinks and one of your friends said, "Let's have another one." Now, this comes off more like a command, and even though it is fairly polite, it is hard to resist.

So you will most probably oblige unless you really don't want to drink anymore. On the other hand, if your friend asks you, "Do you want another drink?" the power instantly shifts to you, and then it is in your control to decide whether you really want one or not.

The waitstaff at high-end restaurants is often well versed with this technique. They know what to say to get you to buy more. So for example, when you order something like steak and fries, they will often ask you, "What would you like as a starter?" And this makes you instantly look at the menu to find a good starter. Even if you decide not to have one, they at least made you think about it, and that's really their goal. Saying something like, "Would you like a starter?" doesn't work half as well because it just doesn't have that persuasive pull.

Restricting the Choice

This is another one of those really simple yet really powerful techniques. It works by restricting the choice of the listener while giving them an illusion of choice and making them think that they're really in control. Just like in the previous technique, I'll give you an example from the hospitality industry.

When you dine in a fine restaurant, the trained waiter will very politely ask you at some point, "What kind of wine would you like to have?", or "Red or white wine?" These questions are meant to give you an illusion of choice, but really all they're doing is limiting your choice of drinks to the types of wine they have.

If the waiter asks you, "Would you like something to drink?" or something to that effect, it might not have be anywhere near as effective. Now, just like in the previous technique, nobody is forced to accept the offer, but the way the question is posed in the former example sure makes it a lot more difficult for the patrons to resist.

Various fast-food joints like McDonald's and Subway use this technique. While you're ordering a burger, they will very politely ask you something like, "Single or double cheese?" This makes you feel that you are being offered a choice, but what they are actually doing is making sure you don't choose the "no cheese" option.

Something similar is often used when dealing with kids when they're being stubborn. In fact, some smarter parents use it from the get-go so they don't have to deal with stubbornness at all. If you are a parent, you must be familiar with it in some way already.

For instance, when your child doesn't want to go to sleep, instead of trying to scold them or asserting control in a traditional way, what works much better is restricting their choice by distracting them with something else. So you say something like, "Would you like to hear a bedtime story when you have your jammies on?"

In this case, having PJs on is asserted as something that is going to happen either way, and the child only has a choice in whether he wants to hear a bedtime story or not.

"I can, but I'd Rather Not"

This is one of those techniques that people often use with their friends and partners. Everyone uses this, and you might have used it at some point in your life when you wanted to manipulate people into doing what you wanted.

Let me explain how it works with an example. Say you and your friends are going out for the night. You all have a few drinks except for one guy. When you leave, you know it won't be safe to drive while you're inebriated, so you say to your sober friend, "Hey, I can drive if you want," slightly stressing the "if you want" part. This change in tone prompts your friend to step up and volunteer to drive.

If this doesn't seem like the kind of thing you would want to do, maybe you can try a variation of it. When you and your partner are leaving for dinner, you can say, "I'm happy to drive to < the name of the place>" and this conveys to your partner that he or she will be the one driving when you guys come back home.

Know When to Use "and" and "but"

You may not actively realize it, but for a three-lettered word, "but" sure is very powerful. It can change opinions in a matter of seconds. So be very careful of the words that follow. If you understand its power, you can always use it to your advantage.

For example, saying something like, "My friend can do this for you in just a day, but she will charge you $100" makes the listener focus on the latter part: the cost of the work. They might think that a hundred dollars is a bit too much for the work, and so might decline your offer. On the other hand, if you reverse the same sentence and say, "My friend will charge you $100 for this job, but she'll finish it in just one day." This will have a much more powerful positive impact on the listener, as he or she will focus on the "just one day" part. The importance of the cost will be diminished and what will shine is your friend's ability to do the job quickly.

So, to get you familiarized with this, here is a great exercise that you can do with a friend. The rules are:

Each person only gets to say one sentence.

Each sentence starts with the word "and."

After several sentences, change the "and" to "but" and notice the difference. I'm pretty sure that they will have very different impacts on both of you.

Find out What People really Want

This is one of the more advanced persuasion techniques NLP has to offer because what you say really depends on the situation every time, but the rewards are also worth the effort. You get to know what people really want deep inside, and so you can reach common ground accordingly.

It's difficult to get people to disclose what they really want, often because they themselves haven't properly thought about it and they need to be poked a little to think in that direction. What this technique does is remove the need for guesswork on your part. All you need to do is handle the situation properly and people will tell you what they want all by themselves. You just need to gently turn the conversation in the right direction and ask them the right questions.

So, for instance, if you're discussing holiday plans with your friends and you ask them where they want to go, they might respond with an uninterested "I don't know," but they probably do. Now, to know where they really want to go, just ask them a simple question: "Well, if we remove the distance and money factors, where would you like to go then? Think about it." This gives them the chance to really tell you where they want to go, and after that, you can start thinking about the factors that do, in fact, matter (like money and distance) and tailor your response to reach common ground. This will help you all go on a trip where you can do what you all enjoy with a little bit of compromise.

Chapter Six: Explaining VAK

We all use our physical senses to experience the world around us. The five primary senses are sight, hearing, touch, smell, and taste. In NLP, these senses are split into three categories: visual, auditory, and kinesthetic. All the things that we see fall under the category of visual senses; auditory includes all the things we hear; and kinesthetic senses refers to the things that we feel, taste, or smell.

If you want to discover the way in which you use your senses, then take a trip down the memory lane. Remember a pleasant situation, such as a holiday. What is the first thing or sensation that such a memory triggers in your mind? Whatever your first thought is, it will fit into one of the three VAK (Visual, Auditory and Kinesthetic) categories.

For instance, if you remember a beach holiday, for some people the first thing they recollect will be the pleasant blue sky (visual); for others it may be the sound of the waves (auditory). And for others it may be the smell of the sea, the taste of ice cream, or the like (kinesthetic). Your first thought about a memory will help you understand your preferred rep system.

The concept of VAK is a handy tool for interpersonal communication. By using visual words, you can attract someone's interest; with auditory words you can catch the attention of the person; and kinesthetic cues will help you build a rapport. In this section, you will learn about verbal and nonverbal cues.

Nonverbal communication is very tricky to understand. What

we put into words is very clear to understand, but our facial expressions, gestures, and eye contact speak the loudest. Understanding nonverbal communication is a powerful tool that can help a person understand others better and build interpersonal and professional relationships. It can also help you to express yourself better and make connections.

Understanding Nonverbal Cues

While having a conversation with someone, you give away a lot by the way you sit, listen, move, look, and react. The other person can tell whether you are really interested in what they are saying or not, or if you are just pretending to care. When your body language is on par with your words, there is an increase in trust and clarity. When your words don't match with your body language it leads to mistrust, misunderstandings, and tension. For better communication, you need to become more conscious and receptive to the nonverbal cues of others as well as yourself.

Nonverbal cues include the following:

Facial Expressions

Facial expressions are all revealing. Your face expresses emotions more than your words ever can. A smile indicates affection or happiness. A frown indicates disapproval or disappointment. You might say you're doing well, or you're not angry or upset with someone, but your facial expressions may say otherwise. Facial expressions for anger, fear, surprise, disgust, disinterest, irritation, and exhilaration are all very strong and unambiguous.

Eye Contact

Eye contact is another nonverbal communication cue which can give away a lot. When you look into someone's eyes while talking it is a sign of genuine interest and understanding. When the other person fails to make eye contact, is blinking too much, or looks away from you it can mean they are distracted, uncomfortable, nervous, or concealing their feelings.

Mouth

Mouth movements are very important while reading body language. Biting the lips, pursed lips, and covering the mouth are a few signals that convey feelings like distrust, anxiety, and stress.

Posture

Postures say a lot about your state of mind. If you are leaning towards someone while talking it means you are interested in the conversation and attentive. An open posture indicates friendliness and willingness. A closed posture like folded hands or crossed legs indicates unfriendliness and hostility. The way you sit also says a lot; if you are sitting straight, that indicates attentiveness and focus. Sitting with the body hunched forward can mean that a person is tired or bored. Having good posture puts across a good image of you.

Touch

Communicating through touch is very effective. A firm handshake, a warm hug, a pat on the back, and a reassuring arm pat all convey various messages. Touch cues are very subtle and simple to understand. In order to understand and send these nonverbal cues, you need to be emotionally aware during a conversation and be sensitive towards the other person. You need to acknowledge the emotions of others and accurately analyze the cues that are being sent to you. It will help you create and build trust and be responsive to the other person by showing you care and understand.

Tone

The tone of your voice, which means the loudness or the pitch, is also considered a nonverbal cue. The tone of one's voice can have a strong impression on what is being said, when someone talks in a powerful voice.

Nonverbal cues reassure you of what is being said. Make a note of all the cues you are receiving and note whether they are consistent with what is being said. Trust your gut; if you think the cues are not matching up to what is being said then you might be right because nonverbal cues say much more than verbal ones. Learn to understand with your eyes and you won't miss these nonverbal cues.

Understanding Context

While having a conversation with someone, make sure that you observe the body language of the person who you are talking to so you can use your words wisely. Body language can inform you about the comfort level of a person, but that is about it. This is where context comes into play. Understanding context means being mindful of the following things:

The Conversation

You must pay close attention to when the body language of the person changes. What was it that made the person uncomfortable? Was it a question you asked or the topic you were speaking about? Maybe something you said made the other person feel uncomfortable.

The Surrounding Area during the Conversation:

Unless you are in a closed room, all conversations are affected by the environment. Look around you to see the reason why your partner or colleague is uncomfortable. Is there some bothersome noise that is affecting the conversation? Maybe there is an argument going on at the neighboring table, too much of a crowd, or someone your partner knows might've walked in. All these things affect someone's body language and you need to understand that not every person reacts the same way.

Recent Experiences:

During a conversation, you have to keep in mind that your colleague or partner might have had some experiences during the day that might have made them uncomfortable and which may have affected their body language in a negative way. For example, an argument with someone, a rough day at work, health issues, financial troubles, and personal problems may reflect on the body language of a person. If they are still thinking about the stressful situations in their lives, they might appear sad, uncomfortable, distracted, and disinterested.

Take time to determine the reason for your partner's discomfort. Suggest moving to another room or changing the topic and see if that makes a difference. If there is no improvement in their body language, then you can politely ask them if anything is wrong. You might think you are the problem, but there might be something else that is bothering the other person. Offer them some food and beverages and talk about something fun and interesting instead of the same mundane topics. Analyzing and understanding context may seem like an impossible task but with practice, you will get better, and it will become your most valuable skill.

The next time you are having a meeting with your boss, colleagues, or even when you're on a date or out with a friend, watch out for these cues to effectively read people.

Smile

Know a fake smile from a real smile. A real smile will light up the person's face and cause crinkles near the eyes. Your eyes cannot lie, so next time you want to know if someone's smile is genuine, be sure to watch the crinkles near the eyes.

Eye Contact

Eye contact is another important aspect when you want to read someone. Eyes are very expressive and are considered a window to the soul. If the person is looking into your eyes and talking, then it means they are comfortable with you. When you are having a conflict with someone and they cannot look you in the eye, it means they are hiding something from you.

Jittery Movements

When someone repeatedly touches their face, hair, and neck, it means they are nervous and are scared of disapproval. Fidgeting with an object while talking also signifies restlessness and distraction. Clenching the jaw, tightening the neck, or furrowing the brows are all signs of stress and anxiety.

When someone copies your body language, it is a sign of agreement and comfort. This is especially a good sign during negotiations as it shows you what the other person is thinking.

Posture

Slouching while sitting, and droopy shoulders, are signs of low self-esteem and confidence. Such people have trouble expressing their feelings. Sitting upright shows confidence and enthusiasm. You cannot feign interest, as your body language will not match your words.

Placement of Legs

When someone is shaking their leg while talking to you, it means that they are nervous or uneasy. This is a common habit especially during interviews and creates an impression on the interviewer. This is a sign of insecurity and shakiness, which is not very well appreciated.

Placement of Hands

The placement of hands also says a lot about a person's state of mind. When a person has his or her hands on the hips while standing, it means they are enthusiastic, interested, and energetic. Hand gestures while talking means that the person is trying to explain and express feelings and ideas.

Be aware of the surroundings and context when you are reading someone, as body language is just going to give you a hint at what the person is thinking and feeling. For in-depth analysis, you have to take into account the context and apply it accurately.

Facial Expressions

A person can convey volumes through their facial expressions. A smile shows approval or happiness. A frown, on the other hand, shows disapproval or indicates that the person is unhappy. At times, facial expressions might reveal what the person is truly feeling. When someone says they are fine, but they have a small frown on their face, their words are certainly contradictory of what they are feeling. A couple of emotions that can be expressed through facial expressions include happiness, sadness, anger, disgust, surprise, fear, confusion, desire, and contempt. The expression present on a person's face can help you in determining whether they mean what they are saying or not. Facial expressions are part of a universal form of body language. It is quite difficult to control facial expressions when a person is feeling extreme emotions. You can gauge what a person is saying by paying close attention to their facial expressions.

Eyes

Eyes are considered to be the windows to the soul. Eyes are capable of revealing a lot about a person's thoughts and feelings. When you engage in a conversation with someone, observe their eye movements. This must be a general part of your communication process. A couple of things that you must look out for are whether the person is maintaining eye contact, is averting his or her gaze, has dilated pupils, and is blinking either normally or rapidly.

Gazing

When a person maintains eye contact while conversing, it shows interest and implies that the person is paying attention;

however, prolonged eye contact can be perceived to be threatening and intimidating. Breaking eye contact frequently or looking away indicates that the person is distracted, is uncomfortable, or is trying to hide something.

Blinking

Blinking is quite natural; however, blinking too much or too little can signify different things. If a person seems to be distressed or uncomfortable, the person will blink a lot and quite rapidly. Blinking signifies that the person is trying to control what they are truly feeling. For instance, a poker player might blink deliberately and less frequently to hide his or her excitement about the hand he or she has been dealt.

Size of the Pupil

The dilation of the pupil is a very subtle nonverbal gesture. The level of light in the surroundings often causes the pupil to dilate. Even different emotions lead to the dilation of people. When a person is attracted to someone else, their pupils dilate. This shows attraction and arousal and gives rise to the popular phrase "bedroom eyes."

Mouth

The movements of the mouth can also help in reading a person's body language. For instance, chewing the bottom lip indicates insecurity, fear, or worry. Covering one's mouth might be an effort made to politely cover a yawn or a cough; however, it can also be an attempt to stifle disapproval or judgment. One of the greatest signals while interpreting what a person is saying is a smile. A smile can mean various things depending on whether it is genuine or not. Pay attention to the following signals while analyzing body language.

Pursed Lips

While conversing, if someone purses their lips, it shows disapproval, distaste, or even distrust.

Biting of the Lip

Shows anxiety, worry, or stress.

Covering of the Mouth

This is often done for hiding an emotional reaction, like trying to hide a smirk!

A slight change in the mouth is a subtle indicator of what the person is truly feeling. If the corners of the mouth are turned upwards, the person might be feeling optimistic or happy, and if they are turned down, it shows disapproval or sadness.

Gestures

These are perhaps the most obvious signals used. Waving of arms, pointing towards something, or using the fingers for indicating numbers are amongst the most commonly used and easy to interpret gestures. Here are a few gestures that can help you in getting a better understanding of what a person is saying. A clenched fist shows that a person is angry. The thumbs up and thumbs down gestures signify approval and disapproval respectively. The "v" sign made by just lifting the index and middle fingers to form the letter "v" signifies victory or peace.

Arms and Legs

The crossing of arms shows defensiveness, and the crossing of legs indicates discomfort or dislike. When a person has a smile pasted on their face but is standing with their arms crossed, their body language certainly doesn't back up that smile. There are certain subtle gestures that are made by the widening of arms to assume a commanding position or for minimizing the attention of others. When someone is standing with their arms placed on their hips, it shows that a person is ready, in control, or it can also suggest aggressiveness. Tapping of fingers or fidgeting with them shows impatience, boredom, and restlessness. The crossing of legs shows the desire for privacy, and clasping of hands behind the back indicates anger, anxiousness, or utter boredom.

Postures

The way a person holds his or her body is an important part for analyzing body language. Posture refers to the overall physical form of the individual and the manner in which they carry themselves. A lot can be inferred about a person's characteristics from their posture like whether the person is confident, open, dominating, or submissive. When someone sits with his or her back upright, it shows that the person is paying attention and is focused on what is going on. Hunching or slouching while sitting implies that the individual is bored or indifferent towards what's going on.

Open Posture

This involves keeping one's torso open and exposed. This shows that the person is open, willing, friendly, and approachable.

Closed Posture

If a person is hiding his or her torso by hunching forwards and keeping the hands and legs crossed, it can be an indicator of hostility, unfriendliness, or even anxiety.

Personal Space

What does personal space mean? Did you ever feel uncomfortable when someone gets a little too close to you? Personal space refers to the social distance that an individual like to maintain with others. The physical space between two individuals can provide a lot of information if you know what you are looking for.

Intimate Distance

If the physical distance is between six to 18 inches, it shows that the individuals share a close or an intimate relationship. This happens while whispering, hugging, or touching.

Personal Distance

This is the physical distance that is usually maintained while talking to family members or close friends and it ranges between 1.5 to four feet. The closer a person stands to another while communicating, the closer the bond that they share.

Social Distance

Social distance is the distance that is maintained with acquaintances. When an individual knows the other person fairly well, the distance maintained is between four to 12 feet. Depending on whether or not a person is well acquainted with the other, the distance between them will increase or decrease.

Also, the distance that is maintained can depend on culture. For instance, people from Latin America are comfortable standing closer together while interacting with others, whereas those from North America appreciate more personal distance.

If you are trying to understand the true meaning of what a person is saying, then make sure that you are paying close attention to their body language. A person's body language can give away what they are truly thinking, feeling, or implying; however, while trying to notice someone's body language you need to be observant, but this doesn't mean that you should stare or ogle.

Chapter Seven: NLP and Anchoring

NLP anchors are an easy and quick way to tune into a resourceful state of mind on demand. There is nothing better than feeling positive emotions by simply flipping a switch. In this section, you will learn about the concept of anchoring and the ways in which you can create anchors.

One of the most important tools of neuro-linguistic programming that you can use to increase your self-confidence, interest, and make yourself feel relaxed is anchoring. It is a simple technique that assists you to alter any negative or unwanted feeling into something that is positive and resourceful in no time. Whenever you create an NLP anchor, you establish an involuntary response to stimulus so that you can immediately feel the way you want, whenever you want. In NLP, the word anchoring refers to a process that enables you to associate an internal reaction with an external trigger or an internal trigger so that you can easily and quickly reassess your reaction or response to such a stimulus.

Anchoring is a technique that might seem quite similar to the conditioning technique that Pavlov developed; at least they seem similar on the surface. In the conditioning technique that Pavlov used, he managed to create an association between salivation in a dog on hearing a bell ring. Pavlov associated the ringing of the bell to feeding his dogs, so the dogs automatically created an association that the ringing of bell signified their feeding time. Eventually, Pavlov noticed that merely by his ringing the bell, his dogs started to salivate, even when he didn't feed them. The theory rests on the premise that an external stimulus or cue can elicit a behavioral response. The association formed is said to be spontaneous and not based on choice. The behaviorist's stimulus-response conditioning formula helps condition a subject's response or behavior to a specific stimulus.

In NLP, anchoring is a form of relative conditioning that includes links between various other emotions and experiences instead of restricting it to external cues or behavioral responses. For instance, the reaction or internal feeling you experience whenever you remember a particular picture will become an anchor for you. The tone of your voice can become an anchor that associates the tone to a specific feeling like excitement or confidence. With anchoring, you have the option to establish, as well as re-trigger, an association for yourself. Instead of your reaction being an unconscious response, anchoring is a tool that helps with self-actualization. Anchoring is an effective tool that helps you create and restart a mental process that is associated with learning, creativity, and the ability to concentrate, as well as other important experiences.

The comparison of an anchor used in NLP has certain significance attached to it. An anchor helps to stabilize a boat or a ship so that it doesn't float away and stays rooted to a spot. An anchor is dropped by the crew of a ship or a boat to keep it stable and hold it in a specific spot. In NLP, an anchor is a psychological anchor that helps generate a response and isn't a mechanical stimulus. If we extend the previous analogy of a ship, then in terms of human psychology, the anchor refers to an experience in our consciousness. Anchors are points of reference that help find a specific experience and hold our concentration there and prevent it from wandering away. Visualize what it will be like, in an instant, if you go from feeling apprehensive to feeling confident and capable while in a stressful meeting when all eyes are focused on you or when you are dealing with a problem. That will certainly simplify your life, will it not?

The concept of an NLP anchor is quite simple. It refers to a connection that exists between a stimulus and an emotional response of an individual. NLP anchors work because when a person starts to relive an intense emotion, and at the peak of that experience uses a particular stimulus, then the individual forms a neurological link between the two events. As mentioned earlier, it works exactly in the manner in which Pavlov conditioned his dogs to salivate upon the ringing of a bell. We all use NLP anchors most of the time and we do it unintentionally. For instance, a big shiny yellow M can be an anchor for a cheap and crappy meal or it can signify a tasty, feel-good meal. When you are driving, and you approach a set of lights that suddenly turn red, it can be an anchor for either road rage or a sense of mild frustration, according to your temperament at that instant.

The good news about anchors is that you have the option of anchoring specific triggers to an emotionally positive state. It means that you can feel confident, happy, and energetic, or experience any positive emotion whenever you want to. To enable this reaction, you need to be able to use your imagination and have around ten minutes to spare. According to the strength of the memory that you use as an anchor, an anchor can last you anywhere between a couple of weeks up to a month at a time.

It is quite wonderful if you are in control of your state of mind. Being control of your state of mind gives you the power to change it whenever you want. Imagine that you can feel happy, confident, relaxed, or experience any other positive emotion at will. Imagine you can change the way you feel at will. If you want to do this, then anchoring is the best technique. The way we react can be intentional as well as unintentional. For instance, if you touch something hot, do you quickly pull your hand away or do you contemplate the action that you need to take? You obviously pull your hand away instantly. This is an unintentional response that is a part of your subconscious mind. Similarly, when something is anchored, then your reaction to such a situation will be automatic and you won't have to contemplate what you need to do. Such an association can be both good as well as bad. For instance, some food that your grandmother cooks can remind you of your childhood. Or maybe, every time you pass by a place or see an object, it might remind you of a bad experience.

The thing about anchors is that they can be both positive as well as negative. Like mentioned earlier, we create certain triggers unknowingly. These triggers can be both positive as well as negative. It is important to get rid of any negative triggers and replace them with positive triggers. For instance, if you pass by a certain place or wear a certain t-shirt, does it remind you of a bad phase in your life? Perhaps you were out of a bad relationship and that place or that item of clothing reminds you of those bad times? If you are slouching on the couch for long, does it make you feel lazy and slightly depressed, and then you start to binge on junk food? Well, do you ever experience the urge to binge on unhealthy snacks when you feel low? This is an example of a negative anchor that your mind created. You can create positive anchors and in the same manner, you can break free of negative ones. **Positive psychology** is the basis of anchoring and you will learn about establishing positive anchors in the coming section.

Anchoring is a simple technique that will allow you to create or break certain associations consciously. It uses different stimuli like sound, image, touch, smell, or even taste to deliberately trigger a response that is consistent. In fact, knowingly or unknowingly, we use this technique in our daily lives. For instance, brands use anchors while advertising. They use anchors that associate their products with a, particularly positive feeling by using pictures of happy people, enjoyment, or even success. The downside to this technique is that it can create negative associations. For instance, if you wear something during a particularly painful event, then you will start to feel uncomfortable every time you wear that item of clothing. If you wear a particular shirt while undergoing dental surgery then, whenever you wear that shirt afterwards, you will be reminded of the discomfort you experienced. Your mind has managed to form an association between that item of clothing and an unpleasant event. Most of the anchors are created accidentally; however, you can deliberately create positive anchors to remind yourself of something good.

You can create an anchor in all perceptional systems. You can create visual, auditory, kinesthetic, olfactory, and even gustatory anchors. A visual anchor uses images that can bring back memories or feelings associated with a color that can make you experience a particular mood. An auditory anchor can be a song that might remind you of a specific event—like whenever you hear a siren, you tend to feel alert. Kinesthetic anchors like a hug or the feel of cold breeze can remind you of someone special or a specific place. Olfactory anchors trigger your sense of smell. For instance, the smell of a specific perfume can remind you of someone. Gustatory anchors trigger your sense of taste. For instance, the taste of a specific dish can remind you of your childhood and such.

Anchoring is used to access feelings, a state of mind, or resources whenever you want so that you can replace an unwanted feeling with something more pleasant. It can also help you control your emotions and reactions. When you can control your emotions and reactions, you can have better control over the situations in your life. For instance, if you are stressed or anxious, then you can use a happiness anchor to access a happy memory that can instantly make you feel better about yourself.

Now that you know what an NLP anchor is, the next thing that you need to know is how to create anchors for yourself. There is a simple acronym that you can use to remember the parameters to create an anchor. The acronym is I-TURN, which stands for:

- Intensity
- Timing
- Uniqueness
- Replicability
- Number of times.

Now, let us understand these parameters to create a powerful anchor. The first parameter that a memory needs to meet, if you want to use it as an anchor, is intensity. If you want the anchor to be powerful, then the memory that you use needs to be powerful. All that you need to do is opt for a strong memory and slightly tweak the submodalities (a subset of the modalities— visual, auditory, olfactory, gustatory, and kinesthetic) of the memory to make it intense.

The second parameter that you need to concentrate on is timing. The idea is to use an anchor when the happy feelings associated with the memory are at their peak. If you do this, then you will be able to generate a strong response. The best way in which you can perfect the timing of the memory before you use it as an anchor is to relive the memory in your mind. Go through the memory and note the moment when your emotions are at their peak.

The third parameter that a memory needs to meet if you want to use it as an anchor is its uniqueness. The uniqueness in this context refers to the stimulus and the meaning that you want a specific trigger to have. For instance, a popular trigger is rubbing the earlobe or rubbing the fingers together. You can select any trigger that you want, but make sure that whatever the trigger is, you can do it in public without offending anyone.

The fourth parameter is replicability. Replicability means that you must be able to replicate the anchor in the same manner that you created it and it must not be a problem. If you plan to use the anchor in public, or you know that you might need to use the anchor in a public setting, you need to make sure that it doesn't include any inappropriate movements. For instance, the trigger cannot be something like touching yourself inappropriately.

The final parameter is how many times you use it. The higher the number of anchors you stack, the better. As with everything else in your life, the more work you put in, the better your performance will be. It is ideal to spend about 30 minutes setting an NLP anchor. If you do this, then the anchor you create will be quite powerful. If the thought of spending 30 minutes on this task doesn't appeal to you, then keep in mind that once you create an anchor, you don't have to redo it again. So think of the time that you spend on this task as an investment. However, if you really don't have any time to spare, then you can spend about ten minutes and create an anchor, but then you will need to spend ten minutes every week refreshing the anchor.

Steps to Create an Anchor

Now that you know what an anchor is, and the parameters that you need to keep in mind while setting up an anchor, the next step is to create an anchor. It is quite easy to create an anchor. Follow the simple steps discussed in this section to create one.

Pick a Memory

The first step is to pick a memory. Don't just pick a random memory. The memory that you opt for must have strong feelings associated with it. If you want an anchor for confidence, then you need to select a memory of something that made you feel confident. If you want an anchor for motivation, then select a memory that you find motivational. If you cannot pick a memory, or if you feel that you have never felt like this, then you can create an anchor by imagining yourself in a resourceful state; however, an anchor is most powerful if the instance or the memory that you use is something that you have experienced.

Association

Relive the memory by seeing it through your eyes. The more vivid and specific your imagination, the better the anchor will be. Close your eyes and reimagine the situation or experience that you want to use as an anchor. Try to experience your emotions as vividly as you can.

The Feeling

Once you start to experience a positive feeling, create a trigger. A simple trigger is to rub your fingers together. So, whenever you rub your fingers together, you trigger a specific memory. The feeling that you want to re-experience needs to be positive.

Release

When the emotion you experience is at its peak, release the trigger. It can take some practice, but you will understand what to do after a couple of tries.

Test

To break the state, you need to do something completely unrelated for about thirty seconds. After this, you need to test your anchor. So, if your trigger is to rub your fingers together, then when you rub your fingers together you need to experience the same feelings that you did in your memory.

Repeat

To make it work, you need to work on the anchor. You need to repeat it at least thrice to make the anchor stick. Initially, it might take you a couple of tries to trigger a memory. With a little practice, you can see the results almost immediately. Work on creating a strong association between memory and the trigger.

Chapter Eight: NLP for Procrastination and Negative Beliefs Specifically

NLP for Procrastination

Here is a simple NLP exercise that you can use to overcome procrastination.

Close your eyes and picture yourself working on a task and the actions that you need to take. Picture all the steps that you need to accomplish to complete the task. Now, see your expression in your mind's eye. Do you look happy and relaxed? How does this make you feel?

Now, imagine the same instance, but this time you need to see it through the eyes of your future self. What will you see, hear, and feel in this instance? Imagine how your future self will feel when you have accomplished the task.

You need to now make this image slightly larger or move closer. Adjust the brightness if you want to intensify the feelings you experience. If you feel that the emotions are fading away, go back to the previous configuration. This is quite similar to editing a picture. Focus, adjust, crop things, or do anything to make the visualization seem more real.

Once you do this, think about the three specific benefits that you have gained by completing the task at hand. You might or might not have reached the goal, but you have completed the task. Maybe this process was a learning experience for you; you might have discovered some strength of yours that you weren't aware of, or you might have discovered that you like something.

Consider these three benefits that you will obtain if you overcome procrastination and work on your goal.

Now, consider the three benefits that you will not obtain if you let procrastination get a hold of you and you don't do something.

Once you do all this, it will give you the perspective that is necessary to work on the task and overcome procrastination.

NLP to Overcome Negative Beliefs

You can start developing your mental strength by setting reasonable goals for yourself. It is not just about setting goals, but about taking the necessary steps to achieve your goals as well. If you want to start working towards your goals, you need to start applying yourself. It means that you will have to ask yourself, even when you are bored or going through some turmoil, to stick to the plan until you have accomplished the goals you have set for yourself. It will not be an easy feat, so don't let it scare you. Practice makes perfect, and this age-old adage is true! Keep practicing, and you will get better! If you have set some big goals for yourself and they seem impossible, try breaking them down into manageable steps that are doable. For instance, if you want to become assertive, then your first step must be to learn to speak up for yourself at least thrice every week. These instances can be major or minor, but you have to speak up for yourself. Develop a "stick with it" mindset. Even if you face an obstacle or a setback, keep trying and don't give up. Start being resilient and don't worry about the troubles you come across. The goal is to keep going until you have achieved what you want. Think of all the failures as an opportunity to learn—and please do learn from them. Every day is a new day, so don't let the troubles from your past sneak up on you.

Negativity can sneak up on you quite quickly. It can stem from a negative emotion that you are harboring within yourself, or it can be because of something external such as negative feedback or toxic people around you. While certain things are beyond your control, the one thing that you can control is the way you feel about yourself and your life. Don't let any negativity live within you. You cannot control what others think about you, but you can certainly control the way you feel about yourself. There are different ways in which you can manage all the negativity. You can start by identifying and challenging such negative thoughts. You can reduce your interaction with harmful and toxic people. If you think you are in a toxic relationship, learn to break free of it. Don't entertain negativity in any form.

Make use of positive self-talk for building up your mental strength. Making use of positive affirmations will help you in developing a positive outlook while getting rid of all negativity around you. Take a couple of minutes and look at yourself in the mirror and say something positive and motivating to yourself. You can say something that you believe in, or something that you would like to be true.

When you learn to control your emotions instead of letting them control you, you are giving yourself an opportunity to weigh your options before deciding on a particular choice. Take a minute and count to ten before you let a negative emotion boil over. It might sound like a cliché, but it does work. Before having an emotional reaction toward something, take a moment to gather your thoughts and react accordingly. You can try practicing meditation as well, and it can help you in maintaining your calm. Meditation can help you in staying objective while providing you with the necessary time for making sense of your thoughts and emotions. Instead of reacting immediately, you can weigh your thoughts and emotions and then think of your next step.

If you are always sensitive to the petty annoyances and verbal barbs or taunts that we all tend to come across daily, then you will end up becoming quite bitter. Also, you will be wasting a lot of your precious time and energy thinking about unnecessary things, which don't matter at the end of the day. When you start spending time thinking about all such things and start paying attention to them, you are making them a significant problem that will increase your stress. Learning to adjust your attitude can help you in letting these petty and trivial issues go without increasing your level of stress. You are not only preventing the wastage of your valuable time and energy, but you are also saving yourself the trouble of having to deal with extra stress. Instead of stressing yourself out about all these things, you must develop a healthy routine of thinking about the things that are bothering you, then take a deep breath, calm down, and once you are calm, think of the best way in which you can deal with that issue.

For instance, if your spouse keeps forgetting to put the cap on the tube of toothpaste after using it, understand that such a thing isn't as important to your partner as it is to you. If this bothers you, think about all the other things that your partner does for you that make you feel good and in comparison, you can certainly let this small flaw of theirs go. Don't try to be a perfectionist, at least not all the time. When you do this, you are setting high expectations for yourself, and these tend to be entirely unrealistic. Try to be realistic while thinking about things and don't let the idea of perfection create any additional stress or burden.

You can make use of a straightforward visualization exercise that will help you in letting go of little things that seem to be bothering you. Take a small stone or pebble and hold it in your hand. Transfer all the negative thoughts that are bothering you into that pebble. And once you are ready, swing as hard as you can and toss the pebble away or into a pond. Visualize that all the petty problems are drowning along with the pebble that's sinking. You are casting away all your negative emotions.

We tend to get so caught up in the problems that we tend not to look at things from a different perspective. A fresh attitude towards existing troubles can help in solving your problems. If you feel like you have hit a dead end with something, take a break and relax. Once you feel refreshed, start thinking of ways in which you can tackle that problem. If you change the way in which you are approaching a problem, you might find a solution to it in no time. Here are a couple of different things that you can try for gaining a new perspective on things.

Start reading. Reading the daily news or a book can help you in stepping into someone else's world, and this serves as a good reminder to let you know that the world is a vast place and that your problems are nothing significant when you think about the entirety of the universe we live in.

All those who are mentally as well as emotionally strong tend to be happy with what they have. They usually have a positive outlook towards life and don't complain much. It doesn't mean that they don't have any problems. Of course, they have problems just like everyone else, but the difference between them and everyone else is that they can see the bigger picture and know that the challenges they are facing are a part of life. Maintaining a positive outlook towards life will provide you with the mental and the emotional strength that you need for tackling any problem you come across. Remember that bad times will pass, and good times are just around the corner. Don't lose hope.

The ability to face reality is a sign of mental and emotional strength. If you are going to overcome a hurdle or a challenge, then you must be able to tackle it head-on. Lying to yourself about your troubles won't make them go away, and you will just end up hurting yourself in the process. If you overeat when you are stressed or sad, accept the fact that there is a problem that needs to be addressed. Don't look for a means of escape, and try being honest with yourself.

Dealing with Life

Whenever you feel that you are stuck in a difficult situation, take a while to think things through. Don't react instantly, and don't be in a hurry to make a decision. It will provide you with sufficient time for your emotions to diffuse and you can start weighing your options with an open mind. It is essential that you do this, regardless of the situation you are in. If you can afford to, then take some time and list the pros and cons of a situation. Make a note of how you are feeling as well. Try finding some positive points about the situation you are in, and this can help in changing your perspective towards things.

At times, the smallest change in perception can make a huge difference. Follow the ten-second rule. Give yourself ten seconds for something to sink in before expressing yourself. Even if your partner tells you that he or she wants to end the relationship, take ten seconds to compose yourself and then respond.

Once you have managed to compose yourself, before you decide on a course of action, think clearly about the circumstance you are in. What happened, and what are the possible options available to you? There will always be more than one path that you can opt for. For instance, let us assume that your friend asks you to do something morally wrong and you are torn between your loyalty to your friend and your sense of morality. So now you will need to weigh the different pros and cons and decide accordingly.

Make use of your inner voice or your conscience for guiding you. Trust your instincts, and you are likely to be correct. At times, the answer might be quite clear and distinct, but it might be hard to do the right thing. Do not let the problem fester into a more significant hassle than it already is. You need to make a call and stick to it. You can always ask others for an opinion and weigh their opinions before deciding; however, remember that it needs to be your own decision and no one else's. If you feel like you are stuck, think about what someone you admire would do in such a situation. The decision that you make must be something that you can live with. Don't do something because someone else thinks that it is a good idea. Do it because you want to.

More often than not, we tend to find that our minds are flooded with a lot of negative thoughts. These negative feelings can become quite powerful when you keep thinking about them endlessly. The problem starts when you start focusing on these thoughts, and they naturally become more powerful. Doing this makes it quite difficult to break free of the mental rut you might be in. In this chapter, you will learn about a couple of simple things that you can do to control your thoughts.

Making a Conscious Decision

The problem is that, at times, we get attached to specific ideas and complications, and we subconsciously derive some weird form of pleasure from going through those issues. If you keep subconsciously inviting such negative thoughts, you will never be able to stop thinking about them. Therefore, the first step is to make a conscious decision to clear your mind and stop it from replaying all the negative thoughts on a constant loop. Be aware of the impact these negative thoughts have on you and prevent them from getting stuck in your mind. Make a conscious effort to stop all the negative thoughts from dwelling in your mind.

Separate Your Thoughts

When you try to stop individual point of views, you will notice that it seems incredibly difficult. This happens because ideas are a significant part of your mental process. The second stage is to separate yourself from your thoughts. Whenever a thought pops into your head, view it as if it was from an external source. It will help in reducing the impact negative thoughts have on your mind. Once you realize that you can, in fact, make this distinction, you can start modulating the ideas you think about. You must be able to control your thoughts, not the other way around.

Who is Thinking those Thoughts?

You need to understand where your thoughts originate. Whenever an idea comes to you, first try to understand the reason why you are thinking that specific view. Realize that your thoughts can be controlled. Whenever a negative thought comes into your head, try diverting your attention towards something positive. If you find that you aren't able to do this, then try thinking about the cause of such a thought.

Chapter Nine: NLP for Fear and Phobias

Overcome Fear and Hesitation

You can use NLP techniques in every aspect of your life. Everyone experiences self-doubt, fears, and other phobias at some point in their life. Even the best of us are bound to wonder from time to time whether we are good enough. You might even worry about whether something you do will make you seem stupid or foolish in front of others. These fears can prevent you from auditioning for a play, prevent you from learning to dance, stop you from speaking in public, or even prevent you from doing something that you want to. Fear is a major obstacle that everyone faces in life. Fear can be real as well as imaginary. Regardless of what it is, fear has a paralyzing effect that can prevent you from achieving greatness in life.

Inaction can breed fear, and the only way to overcome fear is to take action. Instead of taking action or seeking a means to overcome fear, a lot of people hesitate. This hesitation can make all the difference in your life. People usually think "maybe I am not feeling up to it in this instance, or I am not feeling my best and I will do something about it when I feel 100 percent." However, these are just words and that day might never come. A common excuse is a lack of time or the fear of disappointing someone else. There are so many people who want to change their job but are scared of doing so. They often tell themselves, as well as those around them, that they are probably too old to change their job and that it will cost them job security. As you will learn in this chapter, you are never too old to make a change and all the fears that hold you back are nothing more than illusions.

Even if it sounds hard to believe, there seems to be some sort of comfort in not taking any action. Some simply believe that others are successful because either luck seems to favor them or they have some innate ability that makes them successful. If you think like this, then you have a free membership to the club of whiners and envious people. Instead of worrying about the success that others receive and blaming your lack of it on your luck or fate, it is time for you to take action.

If you want to achieve something in life, you need to change and take some risks. There is no reward without risk, and change is essential to growth. If you really want to change the way you think, and you want to let go of all fears that hold you back, then NLP is your answer. There are different positive techniques that NLP suggests that you can use to control your fears and overcome any phobias.

Now that you know what NLP anchors are about, using that technique will come in handy. Once you've practice anchoring, then you can move onto the exercise that's discussed in this section. You can do this exercise on your own, or you can always find someone else to do it with.

The first thing that you need to do is make some time for yourself from your daily schedule and think about an instance where you faced a barrier to something that you wanted to do. Perhaps you couldn't muster the courage to ask for the promotion that you thought you warranted, or you couldn't read the book that was lying on your shelf which you'd intended to read for so long.

Picture that particular event in your mind as clearly as you possibly can. Feel all the feelings and emotions that you experienced. Listen to any sounds that are associated with it. As soon as the image is clear in your head, anchor that feeling to some part of your body.

Think of all the times you had a barrier, and perform the same routine of visualizing it. Experience it, and then stack the anchors in the same manner.

Now, try to think about the frustration or regret you experienced at not doing those things that you wanted to and then stack these anchors as well.

Once you do this, visualize a time when you took the necessary steps and went for something that you did want. You might need to dig a little deep. The specific moment that you are looking for might or might not seem significant. Regardless of what you think about it, it refers to a time in your life when you did something that you wanted to in spite of your apprehensions.

Now, create a large picture of this event in your mind. Experience what you saw, hear what you heard, and feel all that you did. Transform this picture into a movie and see yourself chasing whatever it was that you wanted.

Let this feeling of satisfaction wash over you and as it does, anchor this feeling to a different part of your body.

The next step is to get rid of the first anchor and as you do this, think about all the times when you stopped yourself from going for it. As this feeling bubbles up within you, fire the second anchor and hold these together for a moment and release the first anchor. Now, as you fire the first anchor, hold onto it until it triggers a sense of frustration within you and then fires those anchors. As the feelings continue to build, hold and then release the second anchor. Keep repeating this process until the need to take some action overwhelms you and motivates you to take action.

This is a simple exercise that you can use to overcome any fears you have. There is another exercise that you can try to dissolve your fear and hesitation.

This exercise that you are about to learn was designed by Stephen Ruden and Ronal Ruden. This exercise is known as "havening" and is quite effective.

As with any other exercise, you must first read all the instructions carefully before you decide to start the exercise. If you must, then please do go over it a couple of times to understand it fully.

The first thing that you need to do is think about a barrier that you have and think about how terrible it makes you feel. Once you decide on a specific barrier, then rate it on a scale of one to 10—with 10 being the worst. You need to rate this barrier so that you can measure your progress later on.

After this, clear your mind of all thoughts and start thinking about something that is pleasant. Now, with both your hands, tap simultaneously on your collarbones. Keep your head still, continue to tap on the collarbones, look ahead, and keep your eyes open. As you tap and keep your head straight, look towards your left and then towards your right.

Continue to tap on both your collarbones and keep your head still. Now, move your eyes in a full circle—first move your eyes clockwise and then counterclockwise.

The next step is to cross your arms. Once you cross your arms, lift them up slowly so that each hand of yours is resting on top of your shoulders. As soon as your hands rest on your shoulders, close your eyes.

Start to slowly stroke your hands downwards on the sides of your arms—start at your shoulders, make your way towards your elbows, and then back again. Continue to repeat this motion.

As you continue to stroke the sides of your arms, visualize yourself walking down a flight of stairs. As you walk down the stairs, count from one to 20 with every step that you take. As you reach 20, you can either hum or sing the first three lines of the "Happy Birthday" song.

Now, let go of your arms and let them rest by your sides. Relax your body, slowly open your eyes, and look up. Look up and then down; after, this move your eyes from the left to the right and then back again. Repeat these movements thrice.

Close your eyes and take deep breaths. Inhale slowly and exhale slowly. As you exhale, gently stroke your arms and repeat this process five times.

You can now open your eyes. Think about the barrier you face and rate it on a scale of one to 10. When you are calm and composed, you will notice that the specific block you worried about doesn't seem that scary now. It might not have lessened as much as you want it to, but it still has lessened. You need to repeat this exercise a couple of times, and every time you will notice that the barrier seems less and less worrisome.

You can perform this simple exercise whenever you want to, in any stressful situation. The aim of this exercise is to calm your mind so that you can logically work on overcoming any fear that you experience. As you let the moment of panic pass you by, you can contemplate a rational course of action.

Overcome Phobias

If you have a particular fear or a phobia, then here are a couple of ways in which you can deal with it.

Avoid

Well, the most straightforward way in which you can deal with a phobia is to avoid the thing that scares you. It certainly won't be a problem if you are scared of a great white shark, dinosaurs, or something like that. It will be problematic if you are scared of needles, spiders, or even cheese. You don't necessarily have to be phobic about a tangible thing; you can have a phobia of things that you cannot see but can experience like a relationship or commitment. So, how do you deal with such things? How do you avoid feelings and things related to them? Avoidance is a way to treat the symptom, but it doesn't treat the cause. Avoidance can also at times intensify your fear and that's not something desirable. People tend to go to great lengths to avoid things and this can cause severe disruption in one's life. If you go to great lengths to avoid someone just because you are scared of commitment, you will disrupt your life and will not deal with the issue at hand.

Desensitization

You can desensitize yourself to something that scares you. For instance, let us assume that you have a severe phobia of snakes. Now, you go see a therapist to help you deal with this problem. During the first session, your therapist wanders off to the other side of the room, opens a book, and shows you a picture of a snake from about 25 feet. Your heart might skip a beat or two, but you will be fine. During the second session, the therapist places the book a little closer to you, say perhaps ten feet, and shows you the image of a snake for 10 seconds. After a while, the therapist places the book next to you and you are still fine. After this, the therapist waves a plastic or a rubber snake at you. After a while you get used to it and it will not scare you as much as it used to. You get the idea of this technique, don't you?

The premise of this exercise is to slowly expose you to the thing that scares you and reduce your sensitivity to it. You can use this logic to deal with any problem that you might have in life. For instance, if you are scared of commitments while in a relationship, then the first step is to tell your partner that you love them. Now, give yourself a couple of weeks to get used to the idea before you take the next step. Over the course of a couple of months, you can tell your partner you love them without shutting down.

Flooding

If you think that desensitization isn't doing the trick for you, then the next exercise that you can follow is flooding. Let us continue the previous example of phobia of snakes. The next time you go for a therapy session, imagine that your therapist pulls a lever and you walk into a trap. The trap plummets to the ground and you are fine. You are fine, and you are in a cage. You think everything is fine, and then you look around and notice that you are surrounded by snakes. Placing yourself in close quarters with something you are scared of might overwhelm your senses initially, but after a while, you get used to it.

Another simple technique that you can try is to rationalize your fear. To rationalize something that you are scared of, you need to examine the cause of such a fear. What is it that scares you? Is it the thing, or did you have an upsetting encounter with such a thing? If you can address the issue that gave birth to your phobia, you can successfully tackle your phobia. If you are scared of commitments, take a moment and think about the reasons why commitment scares you. When was the first time you realized that you are scared of commitments? Is there something in your past that caused this fear? Perhaps it was a failed relationship, or perhaps you experienced a rather harrowing childhood. If you can identify the reason for your fear, you can rationalize it and tackle it. Examine your life; examine the fear and the cause of such fear. When you do this, you can easily overcome your fears.

Chapter Ten: Other Ways to Support Positive Thinking

Get Sufficient Sleep

Getting sufficient sleep will not only keep you healthy but will make you happier as well. The age-old saying "Early to bed, early to rise, makes a man healthy, wealthy, and wise" is true. Make sure that you go to sleep early and get about seven to eight hours of undisturbed sleep. If you cannot wake up on your own in the morning, then you can set an alarm. Give yourself an hour to unwind before going to bed. You can read a book, watch some TV, go for a walk, or do anything that will relax you. It isn't just about the number of hours you sleep, but the quality of sleep that matters as well.

Healthy Eating Habits

Avoid all sorts of processed foods that are full of sugars, unhealthy fats, and undesirable carbs. Instead, opt for healthy foods that are rich in fiber, nutrients, and essential macros. Healthy food will nourish your body and will leave you feeling energetic. Unhealthy foods like chocolate or chips can be replaced with some fruits or nuts. Here are a couple of simple tips that you can keep in mind to make sure that you are eating wholesome food.

Have complex carbohydrates like whole grains and leafy vegetables instead of starchy foods like bread, pasta, or pizza. Your meal must be rich in protein because it not only leaves you feeling fuller for longer, but is good for you as well. Stay away from all processed foods and instead opt for healthy treats like kale chips, nuts, fruits, or anything that isn't full of saturated fats and trans fats. Replace sugary drinks with water (sparkling or still). Create a food plan for yourself. If you are interested in cooking, then learn to experiment with recipes and cook something different. Healthy food doesn't have to mean bland salads, so keep an open mind and try your hand at cooking. If you plan your meals in advance, then you can do all the meal prep on your day off; this simplifies the entire cooking process.

Drink Plenty of Water

Water is good for your body and drinking plenty of water will make your skin clearer and will flush out all the toxins from your body. Make it a habit to have at least eight glasses of water daily. If you want to, you can add some flavorings or electrolytes to your water to spruce it up. Slices of lemon, different berries, a handful of mint leaves, or slices of cucumber can be added to water to make detox water. By following these five simple tips, you can trick yourself into drinking water.

Drinking water needs to be convenient. Carry a water bottle or a sipper with you wherever you go. If a water bottle is handy, it is more likely that you will drink water. Instead of sugary sodas and sweetened beverages, you can have unsweetened water-based drinks. Instead of a Frappuccino, have a cup of Americano. Make it a point to drink a glass of water before and after your meals. Set a goal and measure the amount of water you are drinking daily. If you keep a track of your water intake, you will be motivated to drink more. Don't forget to drink water even when you go out drinking with your friends. Don't let your body get dehydrated.

Don't Forget to Treat Yourself

This doesn't mean that you must spend your next paycheck on a pair of fancy shoes or a handbag. Instead, you need to do things that will nourish your soul. There might be a book that you have been meaning to read but haven't gotten around to. So, take a day off and do that. If you like gardening, then try growing your own kitchen garden. Take some time off from this busy world, put away all the gadgets, and instead do something that you enjoy.

If you are feeling stuck with your work all the time, then take a break. Take a couple of days off and go somewhere. You don't have to plan an elaborate or a fancy vacation. You can go hiking or even fish for the weekend. Do something that you have been meaning to do but haven't found the time for yet. Book a day at a spa for yourself or get a massage. Pamper yourself once in a while and connect with your inner self.

Friends Matter

Spend some time with your friends. Your true friends are the ones that have been there for you regardless of the ups and downs in your life. True friends are like a life jacket; they will keep you afloat. Don't get so busy in your life that you don't have the time for your friends. Tell them how much they mean to you and show them that you love them. Always stay in touch with your friends.

Keeping in touch with your friends is one of the easiest things that you can do to enrich your life. You can stay in touch with them by using different social media applications. Make it a point to call your friends once a week and talk to them. It isn't just about messaging them. Make plans to meet them once a week and at least twice or thrice a month. When you are out with your friends, put your devices away. Focus on the conversation and spending time with them instead of checking your phone constantly.

Smile Often

Don't let small issues bog you down or make you feel blue. Not everything in life is to be taken seriously. Try looking at the positive side of any situation. You always have a choice; you can either feel hurt or you can let it go. Don't be pessimistic and learn to smile. A smile is contagious, and it helps improve your overall mood.

Make it a point to smile as soon as you wake up. This will provide you with a positive mindset while starting the day. Remind yourself that you must smile often in a day. Set reminders or think about the things that make you smile. Create certain cues to smile. Make it a point to smile at everyone you make eye contact with. Smile often and the same will be reciprocated. Think happy thoughts and you will automatically start smiling. Try doing this and you will see a positive change.

Enjoy Your Hobbies

A hobby is an activity that makes you happy and acts as a stress-buster. You might like to paint, draw, dance, sing, play a musical instrument, collect things, or do something else. Spend some time doing things that make you happy. If you don't have a specific hobby as of now, then it isn't too late to cultivate one.

Stay Away from Negative People

You don't need any form of negativity in your life. Stay away from all those who are trying to bring you down. Surround yourself with positive people and those who mean well. The company you keep matters a lot. You will be happier if you are around happy people. Surround yourself with people who are successful, ambitious, and positive in general. Don't argue with a pessimist. It just makes things worse. Instead, let it all go. A negative person feeds off negativity and by indulging in an argument, you are just adding onto it. Just stay silent and let the negativity pass you by.

Dealing with negative people might be quite difficult; however, don't let them get to you. If you can find it within you to give them some love, then do it. If you can't, then stay away from them. Be the bigger person and show them love. You never know the reason for their negativity. If someone you know seems to be upset, perhaps you can offer them a hug or get them a glass of water. If you aren't able to do any of the above-mentioned things, then it will be best if you just stay away from such people. Maintain your distance, and be civil to them if need be, but that's about it.

Don't Forget the Important Things in Life

Regardless of how successful you are or how tough your life is at present, don't forget those who are important. Success won't mean a thing if you cannot share it with someone you care for. Popularity, fame, and wealth don't matter. These things are transient, so don't forget those who are permanent in your life like your friends and/or family members. Spend more time with your loved ones. You can arrange a weekly gathering and meet your friends or your family members. Develop a tradition of a weekend brunch or barbecue that will allow you to spend time with those you love. Even watching a movie with your loved ones will make you feel happy.

Chapter Eleven: Maintaining Positivity

Overcome Obstacles

Focus on the Result

If you are putting something off, then one way in which you can change your thinking is by focusing on the result. Think about how you will feel once the work is done well. Visualization is a great tool and will help reduce the anxiety that you might be feeling before getting started. A positive mentality makes it easier to get things done.

Define What You Want to Accomplish

For instance, if you have a goal that you want to write your autobiography, then make sure that you are setting a deadline for it as well. A deadline can be a tremendous motivating factor. Precisely define the goal that you want to achieve. It is highly unlikely that you will stay motivated when the goal is vague.

Make a Note of the Reasons

There might be different reasons for doing something. If you don't have a reason for doing something, it is meaningless. Having a reason will provide you with the necessary motivation. Understanding your reason will make the task meaningful.

If You Don't Do It

It might or might not work for you. At times, the fear of not doing something and the disappointment that will follow can be motivating. Think about the worst possible outcome if you don't do a particular thing. You can make use of those feelings to propel you forward.

Setting Mini Goals

You can always break down your goals into smaller goals. Doing this will help in making your goal seem more achievable. Not just that, but it will help you in measuring your progress as well. Setting and accomplishing small goals will provide you with the necessary motivation to keep going.

Scheduling

Regardless of what your project is about, you must schedule some time for it. Write it in your calendar, set a reminder, and treat it like any other regular appointment. You will not be able to achieve all your goals if you don't commit to the project. If you feel that you are having some trouble sticking to the schedule, then think about all the reasons for which you are doing it.

Marking Your Progress

Create a checklist of all the mini-goals you have established for yourself. This will help in keeping track of your progress. If you feel that you are lagging somewhere, you can put in some extra effort to improve your performance and progress.

Staying Consistent

If you want to be consistent, then here are a couple of tips that you can follow.

Make a to-Do List

Making a to-do list is very helpful. Take a sheet of paper and write down all the things that you have to complete in a specific. You can either do this as soon as you wake up in the morning or on the previous night. So, when you wake up in the morning, you will have a sense of direction, and you will know what needs to be accomplished by the end of the day.

Create a Reward System

Always create a reward system for yourself. Regardless of whether you have completed a small or a big task, you must still reward yourself for completing your work. The reward system doesn't have to be an elaborate one.

Breaking Up Your Workday

Breaks are essential, and you will need a couple of breaks while you are working. It is quite difficult to work efficiently for prolonged periods of time without any breaks. A small break will make you feel refreshed, and it will improve your ability to concentrate as well.

Don't Indulge in Any Activities that will Waste Your Time

Avoid, or at least try reducing the time you spend indulging in any addictive time-wasting activities. It can be anything. Even something as simple as playing a game on your phone can be quite addictive, or constantly checking your social media feed. These activities will not help you accomplish anything, and they just eat into your working hours. Set certain limits. You can do these things while on a break, but not while you are working. Get your work done and then you have plenty of time for all the other activities.

Tackle the Tough Tasks First

There will always be a couple of tasks that you think are tough. It is a good idea to get these tasks out of the way as soon as you possibly can. Don't keep these tasks on hold. Once you are done with these tasks, the rest will be relatively more straightforward.

Discuss Your Goals with Someone

When you tell someone about your goals, you will unknowingly increase your accountability. It is likely that you will finish a task if you have already told someone about it. You get to decide whom you want to discuss it with. Accountability towards someone else will make you want to complete the task at hand.

Kill Procrastination

Figure Out the Reason

When you feel like you aren't in the mood to do something, this is procrastination telling you to take a break. The task at hand can be something very simple or incredibly complex. The reasons for putting off a task can be quite varied. Instead of getting frustrated with yourself and blaming procrastination, you must take a moment and evaluate the situation. Give yourself some time for figuring out the reason why you are procrastinating. This is the first step if you want to overcome procrastination and it is crucial.

Procrastinators tend to concentrate on the short-term gains instead of the long-term ones. Instead, you need to focus on the benefits of completing the task on hand. For instance, if you have put off cleaning out your closet, then imagine how good you will feel when the closet is free of all clutter! Concentrate on this feeling and it will be easier to get things done.

Getting Rid of the Obstacle

Before you get started with a task, give yourself a few minutes and consider the likely obstacles that you might have to face. Then, you can start devising a plan for avoiding or overcoming these obstacles. For instance, you have received an email giving certain instructions regarding the manner in which you are supposed to go about doing a particular task. You will keep going back to read the same email frequently while starting out with that task. This will lead to unnecessary distractions. Instead, you need to print these instructions beforehand. By simply planning ahead, you will be able to avoid procrastination.

Just Get Started

At times, it might seem really difficult to get started with something. Taking the first step might be quite tough, regardless of the task at hand. Just take that first step, and it gets better. When you stop focusing on all the negative things about a certain thing, you can prevent yourself from getting discouraged. When you just dive right in, you will notice a positive change in your mood and this is quite helpful.

Break it Down

If something intimidates you, it is very likely that you will end up putting it on hold for as long as you can. If you can reduce this intimidation, it will be easier to work on something. The sheer size of a project can be an intimidating factor. So, try and break it down into smaller parts. When you do this, the intimidation quotient will decrease. It is easier to tackle smaller tasks.

The Right Environment

Working in the wrong environment will make way for procrastination to creep in. You certainly won't be able to get any work done if you are working in a really loud place, you have your friends around, or you are constantly on your phone checking the latest social media updates. You certainly will not be able to get any work. Your surroundings must help you work and not distract you.

Rejoice in the Small Victories

Always enjoy your victories, regardless of how small or big they are. A sense of accomplishment will help you in keep going. This will help in developing a positive attitude towards your work and will provide you with the necessary motivation to keep going. Striking off simple things from your to-do list can be quite satisfactory.

Be Realistic

When you are setting goals for yourself, make sure that the goals you are setting are realistic and attainable. You will be setting yourself up for failure if you set unrealistic goals. This will increase your negative feelings and you will ultimately succumb to procrastination.

Self-Talk

The more you tell yourself that you aren't supposed to think about something, the more time you will spend thinking about it. This is just how the human psyche works. It becomes almost impossible to not think about it! The trick is to not let this happen. When you feel yourself leaning towards putting something off for a while, you must try and avoid it. Simply shift your attention to something else. For instance, instead of thinking that you aren't supposed to procrastinate, try thinking about how good you will feel once you have completed the task. In this manner, you will be able to take the necessary action instead of worrying about a certain behavior.

Don't Try to be a Perfectionist

Perfectionism is quite a difficult mentality to function with. This all or nothing sort of thinking can lead to procrastination. A perfectionist will believe in only two outcomes. Either something can be perfect, or it will be considered to be a failure. People with this tendency will wait until everything is absolutely perfect to proceed. If it isn't perfect, then it cannot be completed. This mentality can hold you back from not just starting a task, but from completing it as well. Instead of chasing perfection, focus on being better. Strive for excellence, but at the same time, your focus needs to be on completing the task.

Chapter Twelve: Homework

Try these exercises for a week and you will notice a positive change in your behavior.

One Problem per Day

Every morning, select one problem that you want to work on during your spare time. Identify the different elements it is made up of for figuring out a logical solution to it. To put it simply, go through the following questions in a systematic order: What is the real problem? How does this problem obstruct your goals, purposes, and needs in general?

Here are the steps that will help you with problem solving.

Whenever it is possible, try tackling problems one by one. State the problem as precisely and as clearly as you possibly can. Then study the problem to understand its nature. For instance, you will need to figure out the kind of problems that you can solve. Differentiate between those problems that you have control over and those that you don't. Learn to set aside those problems that you have no control over. Think of the information that you will need and actively start looking for the same. Analyze and interpret the information you gather and draw reasonable conclusions from it. Think of the different options you have, both long-term and short-term solutions. Once you know the options that are available, the next step is to evaluate all the pros and cons each of these options offer. Select an approach and follow it. Once you have implemented your plan of action, you must monitor the implications of the same. Depending on how the plan functions, make changes as need be.

Internalizing Intellectual Standards

Universal intellectual standards include clarity, precision, accuracy, relevance, depth, breadth, logic, and significance. Every week, select any one of these standards and try to increase your awareness of the same. For instance, you can focus on clarity for a week, then shift towards precision, and so on. If you are focusing on clarity, observe the way you communicate with others and see for yourself if you are being clear or not. Also notice when others aren't being clear in what they are saying. Whenever you are reading, see if you are clear about the content you have been reading. While expressing yourself orally, or while writing your thoughts down, check whether there is some clarity in what you are trying to convey.

There are four simple things that you can make use of for checking whether you have some clarity or not. Explicitly state what you are trying to say, elaborate on it, give examples for facilitating better understanding, and make use of analogies as well. So, state, then elaborate, illustrate, and lastly, exemplify yourself.

Maintain an Intellectual Journal

Start maintaining an intellectual journal wherein you record certain information on a weekly basis. Here is the basic format that you must follow. The first step is to list down the situation that was emotionally significant to you. It must be something that you care about, focused on one situation. After this, record your response to that situation. Try being as specific and accurate as you can. Once you have done this, then analyze the situation and your reaction and analyze what you have written. The final step is to assess what you have been through. Assess the implications—what have you learned about yourself? And if given a chance, what would you do differently in that situation?

Reshaping Your Character

Select an intellectual trait like perseverance, empathy, independence, courage, humility, and so on. Once you have selected a trait, try to focus on it for an entire month and cultivate it in yourself. If the trait you have opted for is humility, then start noticing whenever you admit that you are wrong. Notice if you refuse to admit this, even if the evidence points out that you are absolutely wrong. Notice when you start becoming defensive when someone tries to point out your mistake or makes any corrections to your work. Observe when your arrogance is preventing you from learning something new. Whenever you notice yourself indulging in any form of negative behavior or thinking, squash such thoughts. Start reshaping your character and start developing desirable behavioral traits while giving up on the negative ones. You are your worst enemy and can prevent your growth unknowingly. So learn to let go of all things negative.

Dealing with Your Egocentrism

Human beings are inherently egocentric. While thinking about something, we tend to subconsciously favor ourselves before anyone else. Yes, we are biased towards ourselves. In fact, you can notice your egocentric behavior on a daily basis by thinking about the following questions:

What are the circumstances under I favor myself? Do I become irritable or cranky over small things? Do I do or say something that is "irrational" in order to get my way? Do I impose my opinion on others? Do I speak my mind about something I feel strongly about? Once you have identified the egocentric traits, you can start actively working on rationalizing yourself. Whenever you feel like you are being egocentric, imagine what a rational person would say or do in a similar situation and the way in which that compares to what you are doing.

Redefining the Way in which You See Things

The world that we live in is social as well as private and every situation is "defined." The manner in which a situation is defined not only determines how you feel, but the way you act, and its implications; however, every situation can be defined in multiple ways. This means that you have the power to make yourself happy and your life more fulfilling. This means that all those situations to which you attach a negative meaning can be transformed into something positive if you want. This strategy is about finding something positive in everything that you have considered to be negative. Try to see the silver lining in every aspect of your life. It is all about perspectives and perceptions. If you think that something is positive, then you will feel good about it, and if you think its negative, then you obviously will harbor negative feelings towards it.

Get in Touch with Your Emotions

Whenever you start feeling some sort of negative emotion, ask yourself the following:

What line of thinking has led to this emotion? For instance, if you are angry, then ask yourself, what were you thinking about that caused the anger you are feeling? What are the other ways in which you can view this situation?

Every situation seems different depending on your perspective. A negative perspective makes everything seem dull and bleak; on the other hand, a positive outlook does brighten things up. Whenever you feel a negative emotion creeping up, try to see some humor in it or rationalize it. Concentrate on the thought process that produced the negative emotion and you will be able to find a solution to your problem.

Analyzing the Influence of a Group on Your Life

Closely observe the way your behavior is influenced by the group you are in. For instance, any group will have certain unwritten rules of conduct that all the members follow. There will be some form of conformity that will be enforced. Assess how much this influences you and the manner in which it influences you. Reflect on whether you are bowing too much to the pressure that is being exerted and whether you are doing something just because others expect it of you.

One Door Shuts and the Other Opens

Take into consideration any negative moment in your life that has led you towards a positive outcome; an outcome that you weren't expecting. Make a note of these things every day.

The Gift of Time

Time is precious. Spending time with someone is the best gift you can possibly give them. So this week, offer the gift of time to three different people. It can be in the form of helping them around the house, taking a person who's feeling lonely out for a meal, or even catching up with an old friend. These things must be done in addition to your other planned activities.

Counting Kindness

Keep a journal where you can write down the kind deeds you performed in a day. Make a note in your journal before going to bed at night.

The Funny Things

Each day, write about the three funny things that you have experienced all day long. Also make a note of the cause of such a funny incident. Was it something you said, observed, or was it something spontaneous?

Letter of Gratitude

Think of someone who has had a positive impact on your life and write a letter of gratitude to that person. If it is possible, you can also deliver it to them in person.

The Good Things

Write about the three good things that you got to experience in a day. Also state the reasons why such things occurred.

Making Use of Your Signature Strengths

Take a VIA survey. This survey will help you in finding your character strengths. Select your biggest strength and make use of it in a new manner. This is a daily task.

If you aren't keen on writing things down, then consider discussing things with someone who is close to you. Talk to yourself about all the positive aspects of your life. Also make sure that you have practiced the above-mentioned steps for at least one full week.

Conclusion

I thank you once again for choosing this book and hope you had a good time reading it. Neuro-linguistic programming is a technique that aims at improving a person's life. It helps a person turn a favorable situation into an unfavorable one. The best part of NLP is that there is no failure. No mistake you make can ever be wrong; it's just a stepping-stone to your improvement. Every mistake you make acts as feedback that you can utilize to further improve your life. This makes NLP one of the best ways to improve various aspects of yourself.

Every person has the potential to succeed in life. All we need is a little push to make us unlock this potential. This is where NLP comes into the picture. NLP is not a tough concept to understand. If you understand what the individual words stand for, then you will know how to implement it in your life successfully. You need not spend countless hours trying to perfect it. Just taking it up and practicing it daily will help you adopt it successfully.

If you want to lead a happy life that's filled with positivity, then you need to adopt a **positive mindset.** Follow the simple tips mentioned here to make sure that you can maintain positivity forever.

You need to understand that you determine your reality. You are the only one that has the power to decide whether your experience is positive or negative. You need to remember that you are the only one that creates **limiting beliefs** for yourself.

You attract what you believe in. **Positive psychology** is about maintaining a positive outlook in life so that you can attract positivity. If you want to attract happiness, you need to think positive thoughts, if you want to achieve success, then you need to think about that success and not the obstacles you might have to face. Use the **law of attraction** to attract positivity into your life.

You need to create a positive morning ritual for yourself. Make it a point to spend the precious morning hours doing something productive and don't waste that time.

More often than not, things don't necessarily go as planned. You might feel frustrated when your plans change or when they don't work in your favor. However, resistance doesn't change anything, and things just go downhill from there. When you start accepting what has happened, only then can you let go of all the unnecessary suffering. You must begin practicing acceptance, understand and adjust yourself to a circumstance, without any conflicting emotions clouding your judgment.

You must live in the present, because that's where everything happens, and it is the only place where you can experience happiness. Your past might be full of beautiful memories, but you cannot get anything from those memories. By living in the past or the future, you forget about the moment that you have in hand. Your present is critical, and you must start living in it as well. Gadgets happen to be a significant part of our lives these days, and social media is an even more substantial part. Your online presence needs to go hand in hand with your offline life as well. Learn to live in the present, physically. It isn't about living in the virtual world all the time; it doesn't make any sense.

Listening and hearing are two different concepts altogether, even though these words are used interchangeably. Listening is a conscious process where you need to pay attention. It helps in establishing a strong bond between people and assists you to live in the present. Therefore, it is an excellent source of happiness. You need to make a conscious effort to be more present while having a conversation with anyone.

Money can help you in buying things, and worldly things will assist in making you feel momentarily satisfied. Why don't you try saving up to 6 months without shopping unnecessarily? You will be able to save a small fortune, and you can make use of that money to travel instead. Instead of filling your life with all sorts of expensive branded products, you must try creating beautiful memories that will make you feel happy whenever you think about them.

Most of us tend to stop making friends as we start growing older. You must always be interested in meeting new people. It will help you in improving as a person, widen your horizons, and ensure that you have a lively social life. Try striking up a conversation with a stranger, and you never know, maybe you will end up with a new friend.

Dreams provide you with the motivation to keep going. Therefore, always try to dream big. Your dream will assist you in finding the one thing you are passionate about. Let yourself dream and have sufficient faith in your ability to turn that dream into reality. You must always spend 5 minutes daily and step into your dream world. Start visualizing about the things that you want to do and how amazing you would feel once you achieve your dreams. Try making your visualization as real as possible, and it will increase your desire to work towards that goal.

Does your present look anything like the future that you have been dreaming about? If not, spend some time and energy thinking about the various things that you can do for ensuring your growth? You don't have to do everything at once. Start by taking small steps, and you will ultimately reach your goal.

If you want to lead a successful and happy life, then you need to make a conscious effort towards it. It takes some time, hard work and effort to change the way you think, but the results will certainly make it worth your while.

The steps and strategies mentioned in this book are all tried and tested and will surely help you get started with NLP. They will also help you stay with the practice.

I wish you luck with your NLP endeavors and hope they bring you success.

Lastly, if you found this book helpful please leave a positive review on Amazon as it is greatly appreciated and keeps me being able to deliver high quality books.

Resources

https://whyamilazy.com/use-nlp-techniques-fight-procrastination/

https://www.the-secret-of-mindpower-and-nlp.com/NLP-techniques-for-dissolving-fear-mental-blocks-and-hesitation.html

https://www.adaringadventure.com/banishing-phobias-and-fears/

http://www.fulfillmentdaily.com/10-habits-to-grow-a-positive-attitude/

https://www.forbes.com/sites/forbescoachescouncil/2018/03/22/10-ways-to-beat-procrastination-and-get-things-done/#346663292902

https://medium.com/the-mission/these-6-powerful-ways-will-help-you-overcome-obstacles-and-reclaim-your-power-b1fabdb8e074

https://www.personal-development-planet.com/nlp-anchors.html

https://www.nlpcoaching.com/7-nlp-ways-train-brain-positive-ways/

https://www.notsalmon.com/2011/07/07/how-to-use-nlp/

https://www.subconsciousmindpowertechniques.com/remove-negative-thoughts-from-mind/

https://www.gaia.com/article/3-ways-to-positively-influence-your-subconscious-mind

https://www.powerofpositivity.com/3-reasons-negative-thoughts/

Cognitive Behavioral Therapy

Gain Happiness Using CBT to Remove Anxiety, PTSD, Depression, and Other Negative Thoughts through Positive Thinking (Goal Setting, Killing Bad Habits And Procrastination)

© Copyright 2018 - All rights reserved.

It is not legal to reproduce, duplicate, or transmit any part of this document in either electronic means or in printed format. Recording of this publication is strictly prohibited and any storage of this document is not allowed unless with written permission from the publisher except for the use of brief quotations in a book review.

Table Of Contents

Introduction 1
- Why Recommend CBT? 1
- The Cost of CBT 3
- CBT Techniques to Use Outside Therapy Sessions 4
- Why is this Book for You? 4
- Welcome! 5

Chapter 2: Cognitive Behavioral Therapy 7
- What is CBT? 7
- A Little History About Cognitive Behavioral Therapy 8
- CBT in Depth 9
- CBT Principles 10
  - This Form of Therapy Focuses on the Present 11
  - Homework is Essential 11
- What You Learn In CBT 12
  - Option 1: Change the Mode of Behavior 14
  - Option 2: Change the Mode of Thinking 15
- Are There Pros And Cons In CBT? 15
- This is What You Need to Remember 16

Chapter 3: Identify and Evaluate 17
- The Importance Of Negative Thoughts 19
- Where Do These Negative Thoughts Come From? 20
- How Does One Go About Identifying Cognitive Problems? 21
  - Step 1: Recognizing the thoughts made, physical symptoms, or even a change in one's behavior. 21
  - Step 2: Define Your Problem and Set Goals 26

Chapter 4: Killing Negative Thoughts or Beliefs 30

Our Thoughts Overview 30
- What are They? 30
- Self-Talk... 31
- Thoughts Affect our Feelings 31
- It is almost Impossible to Control our Thoughts 31
- What we Think is not Necessarily the Reality 32
- Error in Thinking 32
- Thoughts are Automatic 32

Is There a Difference Between Thoughts and Emotions? 33

Strategy One: Catching the Negative Thoughts or Beliefs 34
- Trapping Your Thoughts 35
- Thinking All or Nothing... 35
- Over-Generalizing Issues 36
- Filtering Your Thoughts 36
- Getting Rid of the Positive 36
- Jumping into Conclusions 36
- Catastrophizing 37
- Reasoning through Emotions...37
- Enacting What You Should or Must Do......................................37
- Attaching Labels and the Wrong Ones too 37
- Personalization 38
- Assignment 1 38
- Assignment 2 39

Strategy Two: Finding the Relevant Evidence 43
- What Help do We Get from Challenging our Thoughts? 43
- Assignment 3 44

Strategy Three: Finding an Alternative Thought Based on the Evidence 46
- Case Study 47
- Assignment 4... 48
- Are There Strategies to Challenge Negative Thoughts?........ 49
- Thoughts have One Name: 'Thoughts'.. 49
- Do Something that You can be Proud of................................... 49
- Make Use of Your Worries.. 49
- Verify the Worst, Best, and What is Most Likely to Happen 50

Have the Right Perspective for Your Peace of Mind 50
Provide Proof of Negative Thoughts 50
Involve Someone Else 51
Talk to Yourself Positively 51
Questions That Will Help You Identify Negative Thinking 51
How do You Go about Finding Evidence against Negative Thinking? .. 52
Some Beliefs will not Cause Problems 53
I cannot be Loved by Everyone 54
I make Mistakes Once in a While 54
I cannot Control Everything, so I don't have to Control Something 54
I'm Responsible for Myself 55

Chapter 5: Working on Specifically Anxiety, Negativity, and Stress 56

Treating Anxiety Disorders 56
Cognitive Behavioral Therapy for Anxiety 57
Thought Challenging in CBT 58
Managing Stress Self-Help 60
Making Positive Changes 62
Tips to Work on Anxiety, Negative Thinking, and Stress 64

Chapter 6: Working on Specifically Anger and Depression 68

When is Anger a Problem? 68

What is Unhelpful Angry Behaviour? 69
Outward Aggression and Violence 69
Inward Aggression 69
Non-Violent or Passive Aggression 70

Preparation 70
Weigh Your Options 70

Steps to Take in Managing Anger 71
1. A "Should" Rule is Broken...71
2. What Hurts?.. 72
3. Hot Thoughts. 72
4. Anger 73
5. Moral Disengagement 74
6. Aggression 74

    7. Outcome 75

Types of Depression 75
Major Depression 76
Persistent Depressive Disorder (PDD) 76
Bipolar Disorder 77

How CBT Helps with Negative Thoughts of Depression .. 77
Five CBT Techniques to Counteract the Negative Thinking of Depression
.... 77

Conclusion 79

Chapter 7: Deleting BAD Habits and Creating New POSITIVE Ones 81

Killing Subconscious and Conscious Habits 81
Why is it Hard to Stick to Good Habits? 81

Differentiate Between Bad Habits and Addictions 82

The Science behind Your Habits 84

How Can You Create New Habits and Stick to Them? 85
Step 1: Use a Prevailing Habit as a Reminder for Your New Ones 85
Step 2: Make Your Habits Easy to Start 87
Step 3: Reward Yourself 88
Step 4: Establish Your Target Goal 89

Conclusion 90

Chapter 8: Goal Setting and Time Management 91

Goal Setting 91

Setting a Goal 92
Triggers from Self-help 92
Goals from Self-Help 93
Common Obstacles That You May Face 93

Time Management 94
Seven Basic Skills to Improve Your Productivity 95

Cognitive Behavioral Therapy on Goal Setting and Time Management 96

Cognitive Tasks 6am-8am. 97
Short Term Memory 8am-10am. 97
Long Term Memory 10am-12pm. 97
Manual Dexterity 2pm-6pm. 97
Monitor and Reward Behavior 98
Personal Time Management Tool 98
Time Flies Worksheet 98
Understanding Your Results 98
Causes of Time Wastage 99

Chapter 9: Other Ways to Support Psychological Health 101

What is Mental Health? 101
In the Name of Good Mental Health.. 102

What Determines Your State of Mental Health? 103

Ways that You can use to Promote Overall Psychological Wellbeing 103
Look for What is Affecting You 103
Building Relationships That Can Help You 105
Make Time for Yourself 106
Examine Your Mental Health Status 106
Physical Health is Vital to Mental Wellbeing 107
Eating Healthy... 107
Moving It 108
Have Enough Sleep 108

Chapter 10: Maintaining Mindfulness..................... 110

How can Mindfulness Help One in Overcoming their Challenges?... 110
1. Mindfulness Gives One Perspective. 110
2. Mindfulness Leads You to Acceptance. 111
3. Mindfulness Helps You Process Anger.............................. 111
4. Mindfulness Gives You Clarity... 111
5. Mindfulness Helps You to Take Care of Yourself. 112

How Does One Maintain their Mindfulness?.................. 112
1. Practice Mindfulness during Routine Activities. 112
2. Practice Right when You Wake up..................................... 113

3. Let Your Mind Wander. 113
   4. Keep it Short. 113
   5. Practice Mindfulness while You Wait. 114
   6. Pick a Prompt to Remind You to be Mindful. 114
   7. Learn to Meditate. 114

Killing Procrastination 115
   1. Stop Worrying 115
   2. Start Small 116
   3. Save the Cost of Wasting Time 116
   4. Challenge Negative Beliefs 117
   5. Search for Hidden Rewards 117

Obstacles to Mindfulness and How to Conquer Them ... 118
   1. Mindfulness is a Continuous Effort 118
   2. Be Aware of Distractions 119
   3. Progress Takes Time 119
   4. The Urge to Give up 119
   5. Don't Forget that the Journey is the Destination 120
   6. Don't Run from Your Problems 120
   7. Your Goals may Question Your Mindfulness 121

Chapter 11: Homework 122

Capturing Negative Thoughts (NATs) 123

Working on Cognitive Distortions 124

Challenging the Cognitive Distortions 126

Dealing with Anxiety and Stress 127

Dealing with Anger and Depression 129

Exercise on Goals Setting 131

Practicing Mindfulness 134
   Meditation while Walking 134
   Body Scanning 134
   Object Meditation 135

Conclusion 137

Concerns to Address at the End of Reading 138

1. Being Able to Cope on Your Own 138
  2. Sorting Out all Your Problems 139
  3. Curing Yourself 139
  4. Addressing the Real Problem 139
  5. Looking Forward to a Happier Life 140

Maintain Your Gains at all Times 140

Introduction

You may have heard about it or not, but Cognitive Behavioral Therapy (CBT) is there and has been in use for quite a long time. You may also not know what it means, but you can land on the meaning of the three words to get familiar with this form of therapy.

If you have been to a therapy session before, then whoever was handling you knows about it and at one point maybe suggested it if they did not use it. Also, if you have heard someone talking about how a specific self-help book or therapist helped them recognize their negative thoughts and fears before knowing how to alter them, then you have already heard about the power of using CBT in peoples' lives.

One of the tools found in the psychology store is CBT. The main focus is how mental health and how we behave and feel are interconnected, and how changing one affects the rest. When put into practice, as we will see, there are all manner of outcomes from a broad range of solved problems based on one principle cycle.

Why Recommend CBT?

While it is not the sole solution to mental health and behavioural problems, it is a significant tool that is useful in helping people identify their problems and developing strategies that will help them challenge what they feel and find ways to counter those issues. It takes time to practice but the theory behind it that it is shorter than other forms of therapy seeking to solve the same.

CBT is a tool to help you address the emotional aspects of your life. Here is how:

- It can help you manage mental illness symptoms
- It aids in treating mental illnesses that did not improve while under medication
- Preventing deterioration of mental illness
- Learning how to cope with stressful situations
- How to manage our emotions
- Dealing with loss or grief
- Resolve conflicts in our lives and find better ways of passing information
- Coping with serious physical illnesses
- Going beyond your trauma after a past violence or abuse case

Here are some mental disorders that CBT can address:

- Depression
- Negativity
- Sleeping difficulty
- Bipolar issues
- Sexual disorders

- Anxiety
- Panic attacks
- Eating disorders
- Phobia
- Substance use
- OCD (Obsessive-Compulsive Disorder)
- Schizophrenia
- Overcoming your fears
- Intrusive thoughts
- Guilt
- Bad habits

As you read on, you will also notice that CBT works effectively when combined with other forms of therapy or treatment techniques. In severe cases, that may call for a professional and medication, so if it reaches such a point, seek the appropriate help as you read on.

The Cost of CBT

It depends on how you view it and the intensity of the situation you are trying to solve. For people who can read and understand before contemplating what is going on in their lives, the cost comes down to the price of a self-help book that will guide you through.

On the other hand, when it is severe, and you need the help of a professional, your insurance coverage can handle that if it includes psychotherapy and behavioural treatments. If you are paying straight out of your pocket, then there is a broad range of clinics which either provides the service for free or at a cost, up to $200 per session if you are attending private meetings.

That is why this self-help is available – to help you cope with your difficulties at a lesser cost than the therapist will charge you.

CBT Techniques to Use Outside Therapy Sessions

You are familiar with how to keep a diary or journal, right? Have you ever monitored how you sleep or go out for some fries? Have you ever tracked your thoughts to notice the thinking pattern?

If you have already done that over the course of your life, then you have used some CBT techniques without your knowledge. Here, you will find all the useful methods that CBT utilizes when tailoring behavioural therapy. They will help you allocate time for yourself, capture the problems, challenge them, and then find the feasible solutions before setting the goals.

Why is this Book for You?

We often experience difficulties in our lives, and some of them are listed in the top part of this introduction. This self-help book aims to pair you with some tools that will help you identify your problems and have some skills to manage and manoeuvre them. The tools we have used are based on Cognitive Behavioral Therapy, whose definition and the in-depth cover is in the next chapter.

While reading, you will notice that the book has some intermediate exercises to help you understand the theory between the lines. These exercises will not only help you understand the art of solving mental and behavioural issues but also aid you in doing the homework before the concluding chapter. So, the homework at the end of it all is based on what we have already learned.

If you remember how we went about solving mathematical problems, then the same analogy applies here. The assignments and tables to fill in between the chapters are our practice exercises while the homework is a lengthy exam to help you capture what you have learnt.

Some exercises may not be relevant to you depending on what you are looking to address. The advice here is to focus on what will help you based on what you want to solve. Once you capture the tools that you need to use more, work on them to realize a happier you again.

Welcome!

Do you have any of the problems listed at the top of the introduction? Can you read, understand, and ponder your issues without the help of a therapist? Have you tried other forms of therapy and medication, but they did not work on solving your problem? Are you looking for a way to live happy again without worrying too much?

Then this self-help book is for you. Go ahead to learn the art of CBT, and how you can use it to solve mental and behavioral problems before they become a bother to everyone.

Chapter 2: Cognitive Behavioral Therapy

What is CBT?

Mental health is paramount in the way we conduct ourselves. That is why CBT (Cognitive Behavioral Therapy) takes a step to change how we think, the beliefs that hold us back knowingly or unknowingly, our attitude towards various issues affecting our lives, and how we behave when facing challenging situations, not forgetting the strive to achieve our set objectives.

Adjusting your negative thoughts using this form of therapy does not need to take your whole lifetime. Those who receive it from their therapists know that it takes utmost, ten months with 50-60 minutes per session once a week. While we can view it as a hands-on approach that requires you and the professional to be available, sometimes it's overwhelming to see you juggle your mind in front of someone who is continuously looking at their watch.

> *The idea here is that our mode of thinking, behaving and feeling is what makes us experience what we go through*

That is why we give you a solution that you can use while at home.

This does not mean that you should ignore professional help when presented. If you can read and are able to identify what is troubling your mind, therapists may not be necessary after going to that quiet spot a few times a week just like in therapy.

A Little History About Cognitive Behavioral Therapy

Aaron Beck is the name behind this form of therapy. In the 60's, this man was busy working on psychoanalysis on his patients. During the analysis, he noted something strange and unusual. They seemed to have an *inner dialogue* going on in their minds, as if they had someone else talking to them in there or were merely talking to themselves internally. When Beck enquired about their thinking status, the patients only produced a portion of the total information.

To give an example, the patient in his office was probably thinking, "The therapist is super quiet today. Am I boring him, or does he have a lot on his mind to ponder?" The first sentence of thought triggered the second one, and this is how such an internal dialogue starts. After some time, the client would think, "Maybe my issues are not that important to this high-end figure." At this point, he or she will not adequately communicate their real feelings.

That is when Beck came to know that something connected one's feelings and thoughts. He went ahead to come up with the phrase **automatic thoughts** to signify the ideas overwhelmed by emotions that come abruptly to mind without the knowledge of the victim. While it may not be possible for the client to know what is happening in their brain, there is a way to identify them and report when they occur.

By identifying such thinking modes, the client would then be able to understand what is happening to them and eventually overcome the hurdles in life.

That is when Cognitive Behavioral Therapy was born. The primary purpose was to place the importance of thinking at the forefront of solving our problems. The terms cognitive and behavior are joined together since apart from the mind, behavioral techniques also need to be addressed. A balance between the two varies depending on other forms of therapy using CBT as the main basis, but they are all defined under this form of treatment.

Today, it has undergone various professional trials all over the world in a bid to solve mind and behavior related problems.

CBT in Depth

Cognitive Behavioral Therapy represents a goal-oriented psychological therapy treatment whose hands-on approach drives towards problem-solving. The objective here is to change our thinking patterns or the behavioral aspects that bring about the difficulties which will eventually replace the focus of our feelings. If you looked at the introduction, there are many problems that this form of therapy can address, from sleeping troubles to anxiety, depression, and drug abuse.

Using CBT means finding a way to change the patient's attitude and how they respond to situations by shedding light on the beliefs, images, and thoughts held in the cognitive process. In that way, the victim can focus and be able to deal with emotional situations.

Think of it as a combination of behavioral therapy and psychotherapy. The latter focusses on the meaning we use on what we come across in our lives and how the thinking pattern started when we were little. Behavioral therapy, on the other hand, digs into the relationship available between our thoughts and problems and how we behave.

The following diagram will show you how the things mentioned above are interconnected. We will then focus on it by applying various life situations that will pick the same pattern as depicted below.

SCENARIO

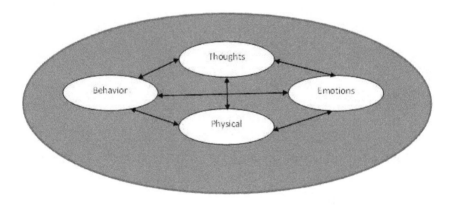

CBT Principles

Since it includes learning essential skills that will help us manage what makes us feel down, you will possess new methods of behaving and thinking as you look forward to controlling your situation in the future. Here are a few things you need to understand when using CBT.

This Form of Therapy Focuses on the Present

We must dig into the past to get the cause of what is happening to us. On the other hand, CBT treatment will focus on the symptoms that are currently driving you in the wrong direction and not where it all began. So, for example, if you are dealing with anxiety, knowing where it all started is not enough to help you cope.

> *Take it this way:* If you are terrified every time you see someone stronger than you, the main reason is that you fear the stiff competition and back in your mind. Chances are that they will outshine you in whatever you are contesting together. If you check the background, the cause might be being bullied when you were young. That will definitely make you fear the mighty ones.
>
> *What's the problem:* Even after knowing the sole reason behind your fear, it does not exclude the idea of frightening every time you see more muscles or brains around you.

Homework is Essential

Whether it comes from a therapist or this self-help book,

homework is vital. Doing the assignments given means that you will have something to do every week and you need to practice what you learn by applying the skills daily. Since it is homework, you need to keep using what you have gained until it sticks in your mind.

Necessitating the need for practice is not enough, so you need something more than motivation. Unless you learn to practice the things you have learnt, what is most likely to happen is that you'll forget after some time. When you are later facing your problem, it will be hard to remember how to utilize the skills.

Learning the new methods can be compared to gaining a new habit, healthy to be precise.

If you need to start jogging in the morning, it might appear hard in the first few days, but after a few trials, it will become part of your routine. CBT applies the same notion. If you make it a habit to practice what will make you change the way you think and act, you'll soon get used to it so, the more you are into it, the easier it gets.

What You Learn In CBT

First, you will learn how to change the way you think and how you behave after thinking. Remember it is a behavioral therapy that is based on cognition. The reason why it is vital is that at any given instance, thoughts, feelings, and behavior are always interconnected. Each of the aspects fuels the rest and the cycle continues until you deal with one or all of them.

Back to our example of fearing the stronger ones – imagine a situation where you meet the person who always needs something from you before entering your neighborhood. The expectation here is too much fear as you ponder what to do. Since he will be on your neck until you meet his demands, you must find another route even though it's a long one, or give him what he wants.

Referring to the interconnection diagram, here is how it would look:

MEETING THE BULLY

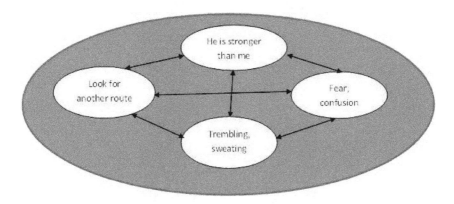

However, if one thinks of a way to settle the matter with the big friend, he might buy an idea that works for him, or use something that will make sure he never gets in your way. By saying something, please think about the legal means, instead of doing something stupid. Now, let's get back to our pattern. It will look differently, like this:

MEETING THE BULLY

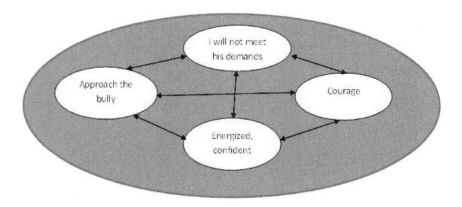

With that in mind, one can decide to use the following options to manage the bully:

Option 1: Change the Mode of Behavior

First, going around the situation to use a method that makes the friend weak, there will be something to tell him and a way to calm everything down on the victim's side. After that, it will be evident in the mind that we are all humans and sometimes we act rationally or irrationally depending on the circumstance. That way, one gets exposed to the person before going ahead to know them by having a conversation that will calm the fear later.

Even though movies are just pictured stories, we can learn this from the stars in the end after they cope with the task at hand.

Option 2: Change the Mode of Thinking

It is also possible to challenge the thoughts by thinking about the reason behind the fear for the bully. One will remember later that it is because you don't want to find yourself in a situation where you'll have to meet his demands. That way, you will be able to know that you don't have to give them what they need if it's not your gate pass.

The reason why we let such fear drive us is that we think negatively on how we have to submit if we meet the person. After that, it's possible to feel threatened and get blinded from seeing the whole picture. Since you are afraid, it is possible to always think about the harm that might get in the way instead of what will make them turn around and leave you alone. If one's thoughts are well balanced, things and situations are seen under a clear vision, which provides the mind with the necessary tools to address the fear.

Are There Pros And Cons In CBT?

While it is as effective as the medication used when treating valid mental disorders, one man's meat is another man's poison, so it may not suit every psychologically-driven behavior.

The advantages include:

- Time taken can be relatively shorter than other forms of therapy.
- It can be the only solution where medication is not working.

- There are many ways of presenting it, which include using a therapist, getting self-help books, or using apps.

- The skills taught are practical when applied in everyday life even after therapy.

The disadvantages include:

- There is a need for more cooperation and commitment since it is a long process.

- Much time consumption especially if it involves a therapist and extra work to be done.

- There is a confrontation of emotions and thoughts here so, during the beginning, one is bound to experience some uncomfortable form of anxiety.

- Complex mental issues may need further assistance and treatment. At such a point, CBT may not be of good use.

This is What You Need to Remember

- CBT is research-based, so there is proof that it works.

- CBT teaches us new thinking and behaving ways. This is a self-help book that can help you with that.

- What we think, feel, and behave are all in a cycle, so they are interconnected. Changing one means affecting the rest.

Chapter 3: Identify and Evaluate

A human being is structured in a way that he or she is not to be confined by his or her influences, whether biological or environmental. Preferably, a human is structured to be actively involved in the designing and actualization of his or her desired reality or destiny, as many would like to call it. This, believe it or not, starts in the brain or just the thoughts of an individual.

To back this statement is a quote from Buddha that states, "We are what we think". This statement means that our actions are dependent on our thoughts – the core of **cognitive behavioral therapy.** For one to understand what emotions he or she has to a particular event, it is essential first to discover what he or she thinks about that event or radically the meanings he or she attaches to what is happening. It may not seem that important, but people are usually different.

For example, a person who has lost their job may find it hard to go on with life because of an increased burden on his or her shoulders, and thus may end up getting depressed. On the other hand, another person in the same situation may find this relieving. This is because maybe he or she did not find the working environment conducive. This person may even adopt a celebratory mood. Can you see the difference in response to the same situation?

The one thing that one notices from the above example is that the effect of an event can simply be changed by the way we think about it. That is why you'll need guidance through CT (cognitive therapy). Cognitive therapy gives one a wide variety of ways to think about what is affecting them. Even in the worst of cases, one will have several viewpoints on how one can view the situation. It is like when a person dies and the bereaved, instead of mourning the deceased death, start praising him or even celebrate a life well lived.

How many of us do that?

Information processing becomes distorted when we experience emotional distress

To start with, what is the meaning of emotional distress? It is an unpleasant feeling that usually affects our thinking. Anxiety, stress, and depression are all types of emotional distresses. These distress forms are normal to human beings.

However, they can become problematic when one cannot manage his or her feelings, and this can lead to cognitive lapses. That is where cognitive therapy comes in handy. CT is usually based on an information-processing model that merely depicts the fact that when one is going through some emotional distress, he or she tends to overthink events or, in short, one's judgment becomes distorted.

A good example is when one is about to go to a job interview, he or she tends to accumulate a lot of stress and anxiety on whether they will get the job. This kind of emotional distress can cause one not to be attentive to the interviewers, or may lead one to not answer questions correctly.

Some may ask how emotional distresses affect our thoughts and decisions. This is a relatively simple question to answer. The psychological state of a person can change his or her brain in many ways. The first way is by altering the hormones and neurotransmitters that we rely on to think. These can be modified negatively, making one not think clearly. The second way is through sleep, fatigue, and maybe even headaches.

However, this is usually indirect on the latter.

Dangerous as it may seem, one can be taught how to manage his or her distresses. The primary way to do this is by undergoing cognitive therapy. CT teaches clients first to identify and correct errors associated with these types of judgments. Other recommendable ways to manage these feelings include spending more time with loved ones, indulging in exercises, or having a proper diet every day.

The Importance Of Negative Thoughts

Just as mentioned in the beginning, cognitive behavioral therapy is based on a theory that 'it is not events that determine our feelings but rather the meaning we attach to these events.' This means that if one's thoughts are too negative, they can hinder one from making clear and reliable decisions.

A good example is a student who has not got good grades in a test. This goes without saying that it will make the student get depressed and stressed. However, the decision that the student will make will be determined by how he or she thinks of such an event. Positive thoughts will prepare the student to see that failure as a stepping stone to a higher grade, and thus he or she will work even harder to achieve more.

On the other hand, **negative thoughts** will lead a student to think entirely different about himself or herself or even maybe the world. The student may start thinking that he or she is not capable of anything in life, and this kind of thought often causes one to go to the extreme of committing suicide.

However, strange as it might sound, negative thoughts usually do have some importance. At a closer look, pessimists typically do not face the reality of life as it is. Instead, they try to run away from the fact of life.

Let's take the example above. The student may have decided to have "thought positively" and ask himself or herself "what is the worst that could ever happen?" and later act as if that is the most inspiring advice he or she has ever got. However, this would not be of help because such positive thoughts tend to show us that we have already achieved and thus make us reluctant. The opinion, therefore, does not make us reach or achieve our full potential in life.

Where Do These Negative Thoughts Come From?

It is believed that negative thoughts usually come from beliefs that one was taught during childhood. We then grow up with these beliefs deeply inscribed in us, and they become relatively fixed and automatic. How is this possible?

Let's take for example a child who has been brought up with the virtue that for him or her to be successful in life, he or she must pass in their tests in school. This is a phrase that is quite common for everyone. The expression, however, leads to increased stress in a child because once the child maybe fails, then he or she will start having the negative thoughts of "maybe I am not good enough" or "am I even going to succeed in life after all?" These are some of the negative thoughts that we are talking about. These thoughts often occur naturally and automatically due to the beliefs.

In such cases, a change of beliefs is usually the best cause of action to take to remedy such thoughts. This is where cognitive therapy usually comes in. Cognitive behavioral therapy helps one "think outside the box" in such instances. In the case of the child above, he or she will be able to step out and explore other causes of action to take in case of a test failure.

What is essential to understand in this section is that adverse events are always bound to happen, but the question to ask is how are you going to approach the confrontation?

How Does One Go About Identifying Cognitive Problems?

To start with, cognitive problems, just as you may have noticed, are issues that an individual may encounter with their memory or thinking. There are two ways an individual can deal with such impairments.

Step 1: Recognizing the thoughts made, physical symptoms, or even a change in one's behavior.

Cognitive therapy usually calls for a step by step breakdown of actions to take with the motive of dealing with a cognitive problem. This is because one can take some time while dealing with a problem. Therefore, the breakdown of a plan into small manageable goals is usually indispensable.

A good example to back up this statement is in the case of a test failure by a student. It might prove hard for the student to move directly from the low grade to the higher one. However, it is much easier and more realistic for the student to move from one rank to another until he or she reaches the desired level.

In this step, therefore, one has to evaluate their thoughts, physical symptoms, and even a change in their behavior. Eventually, this will be able to help one ascertain whether or not they are under some emotional distress or not.

To understand this better, we are going to deal with one at a time.

THOUGHTS

These are the things that one thinks about during an event. When one is depressed or anxious, amongst other issues, various thoughts usually cross one's mind. These thoughts typically depend on the situation. The thoughts we are concerned with here are majorly the negative thoughts. They may include:

- I am a failure.
- This is not meant for me.
- I will not succeed.
- I am weak.

When you realize you are having such thoughts, you are under some distress of some kind that is clouding your judgment. How does one get to the bottom of it?

An example of this is by maybe considering:

- What happened?
- What did you think about the situation?

- Was it correct or not?

Try to answer what is causing what you are thinking. Finally, evaluate the answer and compare it to the judgment you would have made while in a sober state or rather the decision you would have come to if the current problem did not tamper the mind.

PHYSICAL SYMPTOMS

The next thing one must check for is the physical symptoms. The physical symptoms we are talking about include:

- Restlessness
- Lack of sleep
- Increased heartbeat
- That feeling of butterflies in the stomach

A majority of people have encountered a number of these physical symptoms, and the leading cause is emotional distress. Therefore, when one notices such problems, be sure that you are under some difficulty, maybe stress or even depression.

A good example is like in the cases of anxiety and stress, where the adrenaline in one's body can cause one to feel hot, sweaty, an increased rate in heartbeat, difficulty in breathing, shaky, increased urge to go to the toilet, and even butterflies in the stomach which could lead to stomach discomfort. On the other hand, in the cases of depression, one feels tired, exhausted, lack of sleep, or even lacks interest in sex.

BEHAVIORAL CHANGE

The last thing that will help one ascertain whether they are under some emotional distress is a change in behavior. Stress and depression are usually associated with some responses which include:

- Distancing oneself from friends and family
- Lack of self-motivation
- A tendency to eat less

An excellent example of this is in the case of depression; one may decide to stay in bed and pull the covers over their head, choose not to go out, not to answer the phone, watch television, or even decline a friend's invite without a solid reason. On the other hand, in the case of anger, one can shout at someone, throw or aimlessly vandalize things around him, beat up someone or something.

Even though we have discussed each factor separately, they are all usually intertwined at some point. Look at it this way, the thought that one is a failure can lead to increased stress which may cause the person to become restless and thus lead to a lack of sleep. The notion that one is a failure may even lead to one thinking that they are not meant to socialize with certain people, and therefore one distances himself or herself with the outside world.

Thus, there is a cycle of negative thoughts, changes in behaviour, and physical symptoms that will keep you emotionally distressed. We will see as we go on.

In the space below, fill in your thoughts, behaviour, and physical symptoms from a situation you are going through.

Thoughts	Behaviour	Physical Symptoms

Now, after writing them down, try to look for the link and write it down in the space below.

Link between your thoughts, behaviour, and physical symptoms

Step 2: Define Your Problem and Set Goals

This step usually follows after one has determined whether he or she has a cognitive problem, as in step one. This step, therefore, helps one define the problem and, most importantly, accept the challenge. While describing the problem, one has to be sober and of clear mind to determine the problem precisely. Instead of just saying that the problem is the stress, one should go more in-depth and establish the cause of your stress. There are several parameters that one should consider while identifying the problem, like:

- What causes the problem?
- Why does the problem affect me?
- When does the problem affect me most?
- Where does the problem occur?

Once you ask yourself these questions, then you will have achieved the second step in dealing with cognitive problems.

In the space provided below, fill in the problems that you have been facing. It could be one or many. In the boxes below each problem, rate the problem in the first box before addressing it, with a scale of 1-10 with satisfaction going up the ladder. Rate it again in the second box after pursuing it, then the last one after one last pursuit to how the progress is moving along.

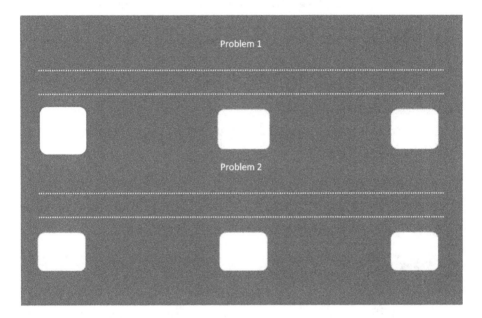

Identification and evaluation, however, does not end here. One must accept the fact that he or she is facing a particular problem and thus face it head on to solve it.

The best way, therefore, is by setting goals. A goal, here, is what the patient wants to achieve by the end of the therapy. Remember that as you read this, you are the therapist helping yourself to get better. A goal helps in remaining loyal to the course and going ahead to check on the progress for some feedback.

The one trick with setting goals is that one must be as transparent as possible. Instead of saying that by the end of the therapy you want to feel less depressed, be more precise and note down what you would want to do once you are less depressed. Some examples are:

- I would want to go for a road trip somewhere
- I would like to have a cup of coffee quietly
- I would like to visit a specific place

These goals can be very enticing while writing them down, but it is good to have just a few goals so as not to make it cumbersome while achieving them.

Now, write down your goals in the space below and rate them after every month in the boxes below depending on how you are progressing to achieve them. Use the scale of 1-10.

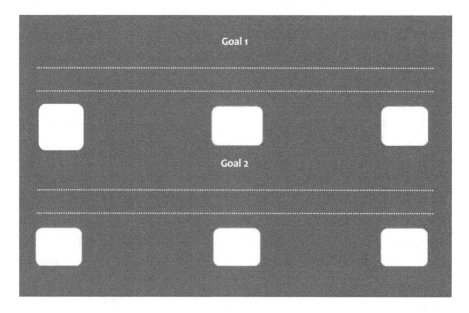

After all of the above has been done, then you will have successfully moved a significant step towards healing oneself. Acting as your therapist is not comfortable, but following the steps carefully makes you conquer your liabilities. Just like that.

> This is the primary objective of this book. To help you treat yourself at the comfort of your home while the therapist watches subtly.

Before concluding this chapter, cognitive impairment is majorly a disease that affects the elderly due to a condition called dementia. However, this does not rule out the fact that it may affect anyone irrespective of their age. Therefore, older people should be treated with much more care. This condition can, however, be avoided by maybe avoiding major head injuries and even regularly exercising one's brain. It can be done by indulging in brain games like chess or solving puzzles.

Chapter 4: Killing Negative Thoughts or Beliefs

Changing our old habits needs us to examine more of what we think. To manage what we need to change, we need to check the aspect of negative thinking and how it affects our daily decision-making.

Only then will the victimized find glory by shedding off the negative thoughts and creating room for new positive ones. At that point, we can now begin to condition the brain to adapt to the new positive environment.

It is essential to address the issue of negative automatic thoughts (NATs). Before that, here is an overview of thoughts and other things that go on in our minds.

Our Thoughts Overview

What are They?

They are what go through our minds. They include what we believe in, the standards we want to live by, our ethics and morals, what we believe to be, and what the world feeds us.

Self-Talk

We are not always aware of this, but we always store and interpret what goes on in our lives. People constantly think about what surrounds or affects them as if there is someone else inside who is communicating to them. Those who are good in psychology will say that the inner voice we hear is 'self-talk.' It happens in all of us, but within our minds so, it deserves the name. Self-talk involves the conscious thoughts and unconscious ones too.

Thoughts Affect our Feelings

What we hold in our minds, from attitude to beliefs, have a significant effect on how we interpret what happens in our lives. In short, our feelings are depicted by our thoughts. If one learns how to stay positive based on the associated motivations that nature provides, there will be much pleasure to enjoy afterwards. Vice versa will happen too if we engage in negative thoughts.

It is almost Impossible to Control our Thoughts

Whether you want to shut out the bad thought or not, just like good ones, it will come and go. Thoughts are merely what you are interpreting from the outside world, and they will be moving in and out as long as you are awake and alive.

What we Think is not Necessarily the Reality

We learn from the environment and our interpretation of what we see. With that, there is a reason why we should not trust what we think 100%. There are individual biases to our experiences in life that will also influence our thinking and interpretation. We eventually attach what we have resulted to meanings of the happening, future or past events, but that does not mean that what we know is correct.

Error in Thinking

Sometimes, we think about the wrong thing – it could be long-term or something that pops up from time to time. Such thoughts will prevent you from making the right scrutiny in what you go through; hence, the wrong decision. That is when you see yourself appearing on the wrong road to decision making, thinking irrationally and judging fast, or even worse, assuming the worst-case scenarios. Such errors in thinking are also known as cognitive distortions since they come with twisted perspectives on how to deal with things.

Thoughts are Automatic

This is where the **Negative Automatic Thoughts** come in – as part of automatic views. They always pop into our heads without our knowledge, and they have no warning either. They are distorted forms of thinking, and they provide unhelpful ways of thinking and interpreting events. That is why they are **harmful.** Most of us who suffer from such will not know when they come and may not even be aware that they are actually negative. If they are frequent, they become familiar to the person to the point of not questioning them on whether they are helpful or appropriate in the first place.

Here is an example of NATs:

- "Everybody hates me."
- "Nothing is ever right no matter what I do."
- "I will lose the opportunity if I'm late."
- "I don't think I'm intelligent."

Is There a Difference Between Thoughts and Emotions?

Yes, there is a difference. Thoughts come in structures, so you can view that as they come in a sentence or a statement. You think about a combination of factors back in the mind before the final thought comes out, and that is why it involves some things.

Emotions are different in that we describe them using one word, angry or depressed. So, people who are anxious are experiencing that as a feeling and not as a thought. Some statements from back in the mind are leading to anxiousness.

Now, we need to focus on how we can change the negative thinking to a positive one and sticking there. We need to let go of the negativity in our brains so that there is room for better and honest thoughts.

Here, we are going to deploy three strategies in dealing with our thoughts. You can call them the thought challenging techniques.

- Strategy one: Catching the negative thoughts or beliefs
- Strategy two: Finding the relevant evidence
- Strategy three: Finding an alternative view based on the evidence

Now, let us see how these strategies work.

Strategy One: Catching the Negative Thoughts or Beliefs

We are not used to capturing the negative thoughts, especially if they just pop in and go. That is why it can be hard to do so. With that, we need to find time to practice this technique so that we can record them whenever they appear. In case you have more than one thought that is disturbing you, try to see which thought causes the 'bad thought.' When you have it, see how firmly you believe in it using a scale of 0-100%.

So that you can capture your thoughts, here are some questions that you need to ask yourself. You can go ahead and formulate such questions for your thoughts.

What are your surroundings?

- What was the activity before thinking?
- Who was around at the time?
- What were you thinking at that time?

- What is the worst thing you have ever thought about?
- What picture does it draw about you in case it's true?

Now, as you try to capture the NATs, here is something that you need to remember:

- They appear as short instances, and they are also particular
- They come in rapidly after a situation or event
- They mostly come in words or images
- You don't think that way from a careful perspective
- There is no particular order in which they occur
- At the time of thinking, they can appear as reasonable

Trapping Your Thoughts

As you try to capture NATs, it is possible to identify the theme of negative thinking. If you haven't heard of cognitive distortions and what they are, here is a description for you:

Thinking All or Nothing

This is where everything is this or that. Nothing in the middle. Something is either done to the level best, or it is a total mess. It may also apply to people where you either love someone entirely or hate them.

Over-Generalizing Issues

If you see something going south and you don't like it at all, you attach the same results to all other similar events. It also happens to people, where if someone is vindictive, you interpret that all people who look like him appear that way.

Filtering Your Thoughts

This happens when you take a particular situation and dwell on the negative side of things for a long time. That makes you equalize everything that occurs as negative.

Getting Rid of the Positive

Here, you shun out every real detail that is vital to what you are experiencing since you see them as not helpful for one reason or the other. That way, you stick to a negative form of thinking that contradicts your daily experiences.

Jumping into Conclusions

It involves making adverse decisions even with no absolute facts that support what you have concluded. It also includes weird mind reading where you reach a decision such as people are not reacting positively towards you, but you don't go ahead to follow up on what's the matter. At times, it comes to foretelling that events will turn out negative basing your prediction as a fact.

Catastrophizing

After thinking that something is entirely wrong, it is possible to start exaggerating the essence of the situation. That is where you arrive at constraining your achievements or capabilities.

Reasoning through Emotions

Since you have some negative feelings, you associate that with the way things appear. If you think that you can't achieve something, then you go ahead and believe that it is entirely impossible.

Enacting What You Should or Must Do

Moving towards setting objectives of what you think you should be doing. They are often high and unachievable despite the force you use to push yourself. If you don't achieve, where in most cases that is what happens, you find yourself overcoming to guilt. It also happens when you direct the **must and should** phrases to people, and in the end, you feel angry and frustrated.

Attaching Labels and the Wrong Ones too

It is a form of generalization that goes to the extreme ends. Instead of seeing your faults, you give yourself a label that you are the worst. If someone's behavior is not the best and it agitates you, you move on by giving them a tag, 'he is just weird.' When it comes to attaching the wrong tag, you tend to use language that is always loaded with emotions.

Personalization

You see yourself as the cause of some negative action in an event or the cause of the whole negative situation. Most likely, you are not even associated with what happened, despite naming yourself as the main culprit.

Assignment 1

Think about the unhelpful ways you think about or use to think negatively. Do you notice a pattern?

My unhelpful thinking ways

What will you do the next time you notice their presence?

I will try to...

Assignment 2

So that we can successfully capture our negative thoughts and see how they affect our emotions and behavior, we need a diary to hold them accountable every time they appear.

On the following page is a personal diary for you to fill in. We will start with an example first.

Situation	Emotions	Catching NATs
What location? *What was the activity?* *Who was present?* *Time of occurrence?*	*What are your feelings?* *Intensity by percentage*	*What popped up in your mind?* *What bad things do you think will happen?* *Intensity by percentage* *Can you associate it with an unhelpful way of thinking?*
I did not finish my work today. I had three days to do it.	Low by 90% Stressed by 100% Confused by 80%	I will not get through this – 70% I'm a terrible worker – 80% I should tell my boss that I cannot make it up to him – 75% I'm a total failure – 95%

You can fill in yours, using the example in the previous page.

Situation	Emotions	Catching NATs
What location? *What was the activity?* *Who was present?* *Time of occurrence?*	*What are your feelings?* *Intensity by percentage*	*What popped up in your mind?* *What bad things do you think will happen?* *What is the overall image on you?* *Intensity by percentage* *Can you associate it with an unhelpful way of thinking?*

Strategy Two: Finding the Relevant Evidence

After capturing the NATs, this stage will help you challenge the negative thoughts. The process of confrontation is based on checking the evidence against and for a particular thought.

Here are some questions that you can ask yourself in your evidence quest:

- What view would someone else share about the same situation?
- If I wasn't this way at all, would I view it the same way?
- What other view can a person use in the same situation?

What Help do We Get from Challenging our Thoughts?

Getting balanced thoughts implies having a better chance at functioning more appropriately. Soon, you will realize that you are enjoying life experiences again. We think our thoughts or opinions. There is no scientific evidence that people utilize to arrive at a certain thought and, since you are thinking, that does not necessarily mean that it is true. The evidence is based on the subject, so there might be some complexity involved when trying to prove.

If we get the factual evidence about something, then there is no room for doubt. Evidence based on facts is object-oriented, so disproving it is impossible. We want to challenge our thoughts, right? Then we need to practice a way of looking for evidence against or for the 'bad thought.' The idea here is to work with the thought that drives you to do what you do or causes emotional distress. This thought should have the highest rating of belief. Now, after getting the thought and relevant evidence, we can comfortably look for a countering thought that works based on the evidence.

Look at the following diary that directs you on how to challenge your thoughts.

Assignment 3

Here is an example of an addict who thinks that they must be on their drug or alcohol to solve stress in life and function 'appropriately' based on their thinking. Do you remember the 3-column diary we had to challenge the bad thoughts? We will use that as a guideline.

Negative thought: I have to drink before facing her in the evening. This is too much.

Evidence for	Evidence Against	Thoughts based on evidence *The helpful thoughts*	Revising what we feel *How do you feel now?* *What's your cause of action?*
I did not meet her	I love her, so I have to be	I'm not a bad person and I have to go and	Alcohol craving? 60%

expectations. I have not been home for a while.	there for her. We can always solve issues if I present myself. I have to fix it if I'm to be happy again.	resolve the matter. I don't have to drink to explain myself. That would also cause chaos.	Stressed? 50% Hot and sweaty? 70%

Now, it's time to fill in yours.

Negative thought: _____

Evidence for	Evidence against	Thought based on evidence *The helpful thoughts*	Revising what we feel *How do you feel now?* *What's your cause of action?*

Strategy Three: Finding an Alternative Thought Based on the Evidence

In strategy two, we used CBT to confront our negative thoughts by looking for evidence on both ends. In strategy three, we will be creating a new thought that will act as an alternative to the 'bad thought' and it must appear as a positive working solution when compared to the previous one.

We need to note that the new thought does not mean that it is the opposite of negativity. CBT may be centered on developing positive thinking, but we should view it as helping you to have a balanced way of thinking.

Check the diagram below to verify the meaning of the above statement.

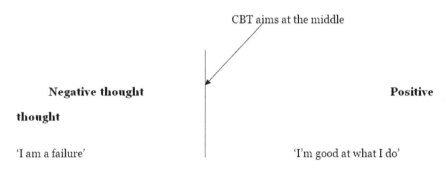

"I might not be able to handle the task at hand, but with the right help and commitment, I can conquer the test."

To summarize how it works, once you capture the NATs, look at the other end of the line and think about the other extreme case. So, it's from extreme negative to extreme positive. After getting the two variables, try to come into the middle by having a balanced thought based on the collected evidence.

Case Study

Picture yourself as a judge or magistrate in court. You have a defendant on one side who is accused of being a peddler, selling illegal drugs on the street. To present some evidence in the name of innocence, he says that he was not there, and he does not do that. The prosecutors are holding him accountable and they have CCTV footage showing him doing the trade for an hour or so.

As the judge, what decision will you make and what do you think about the outcome?

Challenging our thoughts is like being the judge in a case. The defendant can be seen as the 'bad thoughts' which represents seeing yourself as a failure. The evidence presented to support failure is because you just know it. On the other hand, does that justify your thinking? Is it strong enough to live by? Once you consider the evidence at hand, construct a verdict for the case using the evidence for an alternative thought.

Assignment 4

Here is a diary for your thoughts. Find some time and complete it if you are ready to capture some negative thoughts in your life. Remember what we discussed above when collecting the evidence for and against the thoughts. It could be one or many. You can draw a table that resembles the same if you have more thoughts to capture.

What is the situation?	Describe your emotions with one word	What are the automatic negative thoughts?	Evidence for	Evidence against	An alternative thought based on the evidence	Rate your emotions with a scale of 0-100%

Are There Strategies to Challenge Negative Thoughts?

So far, we have covered the most important section about knowing what negative thoughts are, and how to counter them while developing positive ones. They can be hard to capture, but once you have done it, you can start to develop new ways of thinking that enable you to balance your thoughts.

Here are some strategies to help you cope as you drive into the world of positive thinking.

Thoughts have One Name: 'Thoughts'

Whether negative or positive, they are just what they are. You can view them as commercials after a news break or the annoying internet pop-ups on every other page you land on.

Do Something that You can be Proud of

Negative thoughts can be helpful in beating yourself up, but they still come, so you are hurting yourself by punishing yourself all the time. Instead, use the time to accomplish something vital that can help you or give you the pride of accomplishment. If it's something you are good at, the better.

Make Use of Your Worries

Too much negative thinking will drive you towards not realizing your goals and being unproductive almost all the time. You are always thinking about the negatives, but you cannot see what you need to do to fix it. In that case, use your brain power to solve your problems and use solutions that you can work with.

Verify the Worst, Best, and What is Most Likely to Happen

When a situation consumes you to the verge of negative thinking, ask yourself about the best outcome, the worst outcome, and what is likely to happen. That way, you will be viewing the situation from all angles, and also be prepared if there is a mixture of the two extremes. Remember the diagram about where CBT aims – at the middle of both extremes.

Have the Right Perspective for Your Peace of Mind

In one situation or event, there are always more ways to explain it. If your view is not working for you, or it presents unfavorable scenarios, give yourself a challenge and look for an explanation that works. As you peruse, you will land on the one that helps you rest or get on with your daily activities.

Provide Proof of Negative Thoughts

Earlier in the strategies we talked about finding the evidence. So, if you are still on a defeating clause or thinking pattern, go ahead to seek proof of what makes it false instead of sitting on it.

Involve Someone Else

If you are facing the negative thoughts alone, then it can be hard to completely get rid of them. When there are people around you, such thoughts will tend to pop up less often.

Talk to Yourself Positively

The truth about talking to people and yourself is that you'll never talk to people the way you engage in self-talk. So, instead of seeking a way to talk to people the way you do to yourself, allow self-positive talk so that you can increase the confidence within you. That way, you will have your own support team in you.

Now, are you still facing some thinking errors? Here are some questions to help you identify the thinking mistakes. They are based on how to trap your thoughts.

Questions That Will Help You Identify Negative Thinking

- Am I jumping to the worst conclusions ever?
- Am I overthinking or not thinking about anything at all?
- Am I swearing after realizing the general conclusions from an event?
- Am I foretelling or waiting to see what will go on?
- Am I overthinking what people think about me?

- Am I too focused on the negative such that it overshadows the positive?

- Am I shunning out the positive comments and making them look like negative ones?

- Am I positioning myself as a failure and useless?

- Am I listening too much from the negative side such that I can't make time for the positive vibes?

- Am I taking another's behaviors too personally or do I blame myself for overlooking?

- Do I use forceful language such as 'must' and 'should' to dictate the rules that I should follow?

How do You Go about Finding Evidence against Negative Thinking?

- Do I have previous experience that shows what I think is not true?

- If someone I knew or loved had such a thought, what would I say to them?

- If they knew what I usually think when I'm alone or troubled, what would they say?

- What are they likely to say to oppose what I think and to show that it's not true?

- When I'm not troubled or thinking about the negative side, how would I tackle the same situation that I'm facing?

- In the past, when I felt this way or was approached by such an event, what made me cope and feel relieved?
- Is this the same situation that I have been facing or is there something different about the current one?
- If there are past experiences that are not similar, but they made me feel weird or prompted me to do something stupid, what lessons did I learn that can help me now?
- Are there other things that make me think otherwise and I'm not aware?
- What will happen three years from now? How will I be viewing such a situation?
- What positive things can I deduce from myself or from the situation? Am I ignoring them?
- After jumping to conclusions, are they viable based on the available evidence?
- Do I blame myself for things that I cannot control?

Some Beliefs will not Cause Problems

Before concluding this chapter, if one goes ahead and believes in the notion of a normal human being, then the following beliefs cannot hurt you. Actually, they make you stronger.

I cannot be Loved by Everyone

Thinking that you are not the world's darling is much better than thinking of how good you are for people to love you. On our side, we don't love everyone, so why expect anything different from them? It is okay to enjoy being loved, but if someone doesn't, it's just okay. Remember that we cannot make people love or hate us and they cannot also do the same to us. It is alright to receive disapproval at some point.

I make Mistakes Once in a While

Making mistakes is part of our lives and it's vital since it provides a learning moment. Always know that, as long as it is not something that will restrain your happiness for the rest of your life, you will make mistakes and life will go on despite your upset. If you are still learning, then also learn to accept and move on. It will help you change your behavior and thinking as long you are able to handle yourself. Accept your mistakes and those of others too.

I cannot Control Everything, so I don't have to Control Something

We can survive what appears different to us – it's only a matter of accepting what is beyond our control. If we learn to accept things the way they come, then we can love the people around us no matter how they appear to be, and yourself too. You don't have any requirement to like something or put it the way you like it, so accept what you can't change and live with it.

I'm Responsible for Myself

I'm the one who declares what I feel and what to do about a situation or event. If we think that way, then we realize that nobody can confront your feelings unless you want them to. "If I have a rotten day, that means I allowed it to happen. On the other hand, if I had an awesome day, then I should credit myself for the positivity that reigned in me all day long. I'm the one in charge of myself, what I feel, and how I behave."

Chapter 5: Working on Specifically Anxiety, Negativity, and Stress

Anxiety is a word that is quite common to most people, but funnily enough, not many people can define the word. When you experience a feeling of worry, nervousness, or unease about something, or maybe about the uncertainty of an outcome, then you are anxious.

Anxiety in itself is usually a disorder that affects how we feel or behave. This disorder can even cause some physical symptoms. However, if you are facing such an impairment, you don't have to live with it. Anxiety is treatable.

The best approach to take with the aim of treating is to take on some therapy sessions. Cognitive Behavioral Therapy (CBT), Psychotherapy, and Exposure Therapy are some of the therapies one may majorly consider. The thing with these therapies is that they will help you in controlling your anxiety levels and even help you conquer your fears.

Treating Anxiety Disorders

Some may ask the question: "Why should I go through some hectic therapy session just to treat the disorder while I can simply buy medication and achieve the same result in the comfort of my house?" That can be an excellent way to tackle it, but the problem is that it is only short term. This is because the medication will just eliminate the physical symptoms, leaving behind the underlying causes of your worries and nervousness.

Research has shown that therapy is an effective method to tackle anxiety. How? It simply gives you the tools to overcome your fear and teaches you how to use them.

Therapies are usually considered long-term by most people. However, this is not the case with CBT-based anxiety therapy. Surprisingly, within the first eight to ten months, many people are usually okay. The length of these therapies is generally measured by the severity of the disorder, and also the type. There are various types of anxiety disorders like Generalized Anxiety Disorder (GAD), Obsessive Compulsive Disorder (OCD), Panic Disorder, and many more. It is now also obvious to note that therapy should be tailored to one's specific symptoms. A person suffering from GAD cannot undergo the same therapy session as one suffering from OCD.

As mentioned before, there are various types of anxiety therapies that can be considered. However, the two leading treatments are Cognitive Behavioral Therapy and Exposure Therapy. These therapies can be used alone or be accompanied by other types of treatment. Another thing to note is that these therapies can be done at an individual level or to a group of people who have the same anxiety problems. We are going to cover the CBT part.

Cognitive Behavioral Therapy for Anxiety

Cognitive Behavioral Therapy primarily works to alleviate both negative cognitions, that is, thoughts and beliefs, and also maladaptive behaviors associated with anxiety. CBT seeks to blend the best parts of behavior and cognitive therapies.

As the name suggests, there are two main components to this

therapy: Cognitive Therapy and Behavioral Therapy. Cognitive therapy is the part that involves one's thoughts. This part examines how one's negative thoughts contribute to anxiety. Behavioral treatment, on the other hand, examines one's behavior and reactions when in situations that trigger anxiety. It is important to note that this type of treatment mainly focuses on our thoughts rather than the events. This is because one's thoughts determine one's feelings. Let's take an event, like that of getting a job somewhere you never thought you would ever be employed. This event can lead to various feelings which are determined by how you think about the situation. For example:

- The thought that you are fortunate to have landed in such a job will make you feel thrilled and jovial.

- The thought that you are not qualified enough for such a high-end job may make you feel undeserving of the opportunity, and this can lead to stress.

The above represents the same situation but two very different feelings that can be achieved by merely how you think.

Generally, for people with anxiety disorders, their decisions are often clouded with negative thoughts that lead to negative emotions of worry, nervousness, or fear. For such people, Cognitive Behavioral Therapy usually comes in handy because it helps them identify and fight these negative thoughts, thereby avoiding negative emotions that cause anxiety.

Thought Challenging in CBT

Thought challenging is a useful technique used in CBT that helps one consider situations from multiple angles, using actual evidence from your life. It involves challenging one's negative thoughts and replacing them with more positive and realistic opinions. We covered this in the last chapter.

This technique usually involves three steps. Namely:

1. Identifying Negative Thoughts

Anxiety and negative thoughts are a very evil duo that can lead to very severe problems. People with an anxiety disorder tend to perceive things or events more seriously than other people. For example, a person who fears dogs will consider touching them as life-threatening. Somebody else will view this as safe as long as he or she approaches the dog in a friendly way. This step can be tough to take because identifying one's fear is not that simple. The only thing, however, that one must ask is what feeling you had when you started feeling anxious.

This is the only sure way to determine your fear.

2. Challenging negative thoughts

Once the fears and the negative thoughts have been identified, the next thing is to test these thoughts. What does this mean? It basically means evaluating the negative thoughts. Why do these thoughts occur naturally to you? In this stage, one has to question the evidence behind these negative thoughts and also try to identify any unhelpful beliefs that may lead to negative thoughts. A strategy that one may use in challenging these thoughts is by weighing the advantages and disadvantages of worrying or fearing something.

3. Replacing negative thoughts with positive ones

Once you have challenged these negative thoughts, it is now time to replace these negative thoughts with more realistic and positive thoughts. If this proves hard, one may also find some calming thoughts or words that you can say to yourself if you are facing a situation that causes anxiety.

However, replacing negative thoughts with positive ones is usually easier said than done. This is because the negative thoughts are typically due to a long-term belief which needs much courage and time to break. It is for this reason that cognitive behavioral therapy includes practicing on your own at home.

Managing Stress Self-Help

What is stress? Stress is a state of emotional or mental strain or tension resulting from adverse or demanding circumstances. While in this state, one feels as if there are very many demanding actions that must be taken while the resources needed are minimal. The strain or tension can be caused by many external factors like illness, work, home, or even family environments. Funnily enough, even those events that are considered joyful like holidays can also lead to stress.

Why is managing one's stress helpful? Stress can have a hold on your life, causing you to be sad and thus less productive. It affects your emotional equilibrium and also narrows your ability to think correctly and clearly. Effective stress management can, therefore, go a long way towards relieving a huge burden off your shoulders.

How do you determine whether or not you are under stress? There are various thoughts, emotions, physical sensations, and even behaviors that are associated with this form of mental pressure. Some of these include:

THOUGHTS

- I'll never accomplish this.
- It's not fair. Someone should be helping me.
- This is too much for me.

EMOTIONS

- Angry
- Depressed
- Hopeless
- Impatient

PHYSICAL SENSATIONS

A physical sensation is a physical response to stress and is caused by the body's adrenaline response. Some of the physical feelings associated with stress therefore are:

- Breathing faster
- Hot and sweaty
- Restless
- Bowel problems, usually short pains
- Difficulty in concentrating because one's mind is focused elsewhere
- A headache

BEHAVIOR

- Lack of sleep
- Lack of appetite
- One is not able to settle
- Use of drugs or even an increase in their use. For example, if one is used to smoking, there will be an increased tendency to smoke

Making Positive Changes

This is aimed at basically managing one's stress levels. Various steps can be followed to make positive changes. They include:

1. **Identify the sources of stress or the stressors in your life**

It's the first step towards making a positive change. This step is not as straightforward as it sounds. Finding the source of chronic stress can be very complicated. To ease things a bit for you, here are some of the questions that you can ask yourself to identify the cause of stress.

- What makes you stressed?
- Where am I when I get stressed?
- What am I doing when I get stressed?
- Who am I with when I get stressed?
- What change can I make?

Some may notice that there is very little that they can do to change some situations. These tiny things could make the difference you need, so do not hesitate to perform them.

2. Identify the factors that keep the problem going

Once you have identified the sources of your stress, it is now time to identify the factors that keep this problem going.

3. Thinking differently

This step is fundamentally mental. It means that all you have to change is your thinking towards various situations. To help you improve your thinking, here are some questions that you ought to ask yourself when faced with a particular case:

- What am I reacting to?
- What is it that is going to happen here?
- Is this fact or opinion?
- How helpful is it for me to think this way?
- Is it even worth it?
- Am I overestimating the threat?
- What meaning am I giving to this situation?
- Is there another way of looking at this?
- What advice would I give to someone else in this situation?
- Can I do things differently here?

Once you have asked yourself these questions and answered them frankly, then you will be able to think positively about a situation.

4. Doing things differently

This step will help with reducing both stress and anxiety. Why? During stress, one usually feels as if many demands cannot be achieved with the available resources. Therefore, doing things differently by maybe considering what applications are most important can help reduce stress levels.

On the other hand, doing things differently can help in reducing anxiety, in that you can now decide to make time for yourself each day to relax or just for fun. One might also choose to create a healthy balance, in that you have time to work, rest, and do other things that concern you.

Tips to Work on Anxiety, Negative Thinking, and Stress

There are several ways of fighting anxiety, negative thinking, and stress:

1. Understand Your Thinking Style

This step right here is the first step to take to change the negative thoughts that one usually has. One must understand how they think precisely. Here are some thinking styles that may help you:

- If you tend to believe that when you fail at one thing, then you have failed at everything, then you are a polarized or black and white thinker.
- If you tend to know what people feel about you and why they act the way they do without them saying so, then you are a person that jumps to conclusions.

- If you tend always to expect disaster to strike no matter what, then you are a catastrophizing thinker. This type of thinker always asks the question: "what if?"

2. The Ability to Recognize Thought Distortions

Once you are able to identify your thinking style, one is able thereby to determine whether it is a thought distortion or not. Types of thought distortions are like those given above in the first step. They include: catastrophizing, making extremely negative predictions, and also making black or white judgments.

3. The Ability to Recognize Rumination

What is rumination? It is a deep or considered thought about something. Typically, when people ruminate, their problem-solving capacity is significantly reduced. Therefore, it is vital for one to recognize this stage during problem-solving and avoid it at all possible costs.

If avoiding ruminating proves to be hard, then the best thing to do when ruminating is to accept that you are having certain thoughts, recognize that they might not be correct, and then allow them to pass in their own mind rather than trying to block them out.

4. Cope with Criticism

Criticism is one thing that cannot be avoided in life. On the other hand, it can also lead to unnecessary worries if not adequately managed. Therefore, one must be able to learn how to cope with criticism. CBT can help one acquire the skills needed to deal with criticism. During the therapy session, try to weigh out if the blame is constructive or not before deciding whether you can use it or shun it away. Always use evidence to your thoughts so that you can make a decision based on factual evidence.

5. Learn the Art of Mindfulness

Mindfulness is a mental state achieved by focusing one's awareness on the present moment' while calmly acknowledging and accepting his or her feelings, thoughts, and bodily sensations. It is mainly associated with meditation.

Learning this art of mindfulness will help you gain control of your thoughts and emotions. This is because the art teaches one to view one's thoughts and feelings as objects floating past you that you can stop, observe, or even let pass you by. We will cover this as we go on.

6. The Ability to Talk to Oneself Kindly about Imperfections and Mistakes

The tendency of speaking to yourself harshly in the case of imperfection has shown to be of no importance. This is because in most cases it leads to rumination, which then leads to vague problem-solving solutions. On the other hand, research has shown that speaking to yourself calmly can increase self-motivation and also make a person feel much better.

7. Avoiding Thought Stopping

Thought stopping is the complete opposite to mindfulness. This is because it is the act of being on the lookout for any negative thoughts whatsoever and forcing them to be eliminated. The problem with this act is that the more you stop these thoughts, the more they will surface during problem-solving. Therefore, avoiding such thoughts and embracing mindfulness is a much better way.

8. Understanding Your Thinking Diary

What are thinking journals? They are tools that can be used to change any negative thoughts. The importance of these thinking diaries is that they help one identify and determine one's negative thinking styles and thus gain a better understanding of how their beliefs affect their emotions. These diaries are essential in a cognitive behavioral treatment plan and must be completed if you want to capture your thoughts. There are more practicals for that before the conclusion.

Chapter 6: Working on Specifically Anger and Depression

What is anger? It is a strong feeling of annoyance, displeasure, or hostility towards someone or something. Anger usually occurs as a natural response to feeling attacked, frustrated, or even being humiliated. It is human nature to get angry. The fury, therefore, is not a bad feeling per se, because at times it can prove to be very useful. How is this even possible? Anger can open one's mind and help them identify their problems which could drive one to get motivated to make a change which could help in moulding their lives.

When is Anger a Problem?

Anger, as we have just seen, is normal in life. The problem only comes in when one cannot manage their anger, and it causes harm to people around them or even themselves.

How does one notice when their anger is becoming harmful? When one starts expressing anger through unhelpful or destructive behavior, or even when one's mental and physical health starts deteriorating. That's when one knows that the situation is getting out of hand.

It is the way a person behaves that determines whether or not they have problems with their anger. If the way they act affects their life or relationships, then there is a problem, and they should think about getting some support or treatment.

What is Unhelpful Angry Behaviour?

Anger may be familiar to everyone, but people usually express their rage in entirely different ways. How one behaves when they are angry depends on how much control they have over their feelings. People who have less control over their emotions tend to have some unhelpful angry behaviors. These are behaviors that cause damage to themselves or even damage to people or things around them. They include:

Outward Aggression and Violence

This is whereby one directs their anger towards people or things around them. Some of the behaviors here may include shouting at people, fighting people, slamming doors, hitting or throwing things, or being verbally abusive. These types of actions can be very frightening and dangerous to people around, especially children. They can cause severe consequences like the loss of a job or even injuring a loved one or just basically anyone around.

Inward Aggression

This is where one directs their anger towards themselves. Some of the behaviors here may include telling oneself that they hate themselves, denying themselves, or even cutting themselves off the world.

Non-Violent or Passive Aggression

In this case, one does not direct their anger anywhere; rather they stick with the feeling in them. Some of the behaviors here may include ignoring people, refusing to speak to people, refusing to do tasks, or even deliberately doing chores poorly or late. These types of behaviors are usually the worst ways to approach such situations. They may seem less destructive and harmful, but they do not relieve one of the heavy burden that is causing them to be angry.

Preparation

Weigh Your Options

In life, many things may be out of one's control. These things vary from the weather, the past, other people, intrusive thoughts, physical sensations, and one's own emotions. Despite all these, the power to choose is always disposable to any human. Even though one might not be able to control the weather, one can decide whether or not to wear heavy clothing. One can also choose how to respond to other people.

The first step, therefore, in dealing with anger is to recognize a choice.

Steps to Take in Managing Anger

1. A "Should" Rule is Broken

Everybody has some rules and expectations for one's behavior, and also for other people's behavior. Some of these rules include "I should be able to do this", "She should not treat me like this," and, "They should stay out of my way". Unfortunately, no one has control over someone else's actions. Therefore, these rules are always bound to be broken and people may get in one's way. This can result in anger, guilt, and pressure.

It is therefore essential to first break these "should" rules to fight this anger. The first step to make in breaking these rules is to accept the reality of life that someone usually has very little control over other people's lives. The next step is for one to choose a direction based on one's values. How does one know their values? One can identify their values by what angers them, frustrates them, or even enrages them. For example, let's take the rule of "They should stay out of my way". This rule may mean the values of communication, progress, or even cooperation. What do these values mean to someone? Does one have control over them?

Finally, one can act by their values. To help with this, here are two questions one should ask themselves:

- What does one want in the long run?

- What constructive steps can one take in that direction?

2. What Hurts?

The second step is to find the real cause of pain or fear after breaking the rules. These rules usually do not mean the same to one's body. This is because some states of being can hurt one's self-esteem more than others.

To understand this better, let's take the example of Maryah who expects that no one should talk ill of her. Then suddenly Kelvin comes up to her and says all manner of things to her. This, therefore, makes Maryah enraged. In such a scenario, Maryah should ask herself what hurts her. The answer to this question will bring out a general belief about Kelvin and herself. She will think that "Kelvin is rude", "She is powerless", or even that "She is being made the victim". All these thoughts may hurt her. What may even hurt her most is that she has no control over Kelvin's behavior.

Once she has noted that she has no control, she may now consider seeing Kelvin's words as a mere opinion rather than an insult. This will make her not see herself as a victim but as a person just receiving a piece of someone else's mind about herself.

3. Hot Thoughts.

After one has identified what really hurts them, it is now time to identify and most importantly replace the hot, anger-driven and reactive thoughts with more level-headed, more relaxed and reflective thoughts. Here are some fresh ideas that may be of importance to someone:

Hot thought: "How mean can he be!"

Cool thought: "He thinks he is so caring."

Hot thought: "They are stupid!"

Cool thought: "They are just human."

4. Anger

All the above steps, as one may have noticed, relate to the thoughts. This is because one has first to tackle with the ideas before now getting to the emotion. In this step, therefore, one is going to respond to the anger arousal itself. There are three ways that one can follow to respond to this emotion:

- One may indulge in relaxation. This relaxation can come in many forms, like enjoying some music, practising some progressive muscle relaxation like yoga, and also visualization.

- One may also use that feeling to do some constructive work. When one is angry, there is usually a large amount of energy that one uses at that time. This is the reason that when angry, one can break down things that they would never break when calm. Imagine, therefore, how much that energy would do for someone if just directed to some constructive work.

- One may also try to redefine anger when one gets angry. What does this mean? Once a person is angry, one can try to remind themselves of how anger is a problem that fuels aggression and can cause harm to loved ones and even oneself.

5. Moral Disengagement

Moral disengagement is the process of convincing oneself that ethical standards do not apply to themselves in a particular context. In simple words, this step will help one examine the beliefs that turn anger into aggression. These beliefs usually act as mere excuses or justification for destructive acts. Some of these beliefs include "I don't care", "This is the only way I can get my point across", or even "It is high time they recognize me". These beliefs need to be identified early enough and gotten rid of before they can con one into throwing one's morals aside. One sure way of getting rid of them is by reminding oneself of the cost of such beliefs and the advantages of striving for understanding.

6. Aggression

In this step one now needs to examine the behaviors that arise from aggression and try to fight them. Fighting these behaviors can be achieved if one calms down and puts themselves in the other person's shoes. This will help one understand why the other person is acting in such a manner, what they may be feeling, or even what they may be thinking. This approach will help to:

- Decrease the anger for all parties involved.
- Increase the chance of having a reasonable conversation with the parties involved, and thus everybody is heard.

7. Outcome

The final step of this procedure is to reduce resentment towards others, and also guilt towards oneself.

Treating depression with cognitive behavioral therapy.

What is depression? Depression is a feeling of severe despondency and dejection. In life, it is only natural for one to feel less than a hundred per cent at times. This is like when one is battling with a drug addiction or has relationship problems. However, this low feeling sometimes gets a hold of one's life and won't go. This is what we call depression. Depression can make one feel lonely and hopeless.

If one has such feelings, there is light at the end of the tunnel. Cognitive Behavioral Therapy is here to restore one's hope in life. This is because it can help one think more healthily, and also help in overcoming a particular addiction.

Before getting more in-depth with the advantages of CBT on a depressed person, let's first look at the different types of depression.

Types of Depression

Depressions are of various kinds. They can either occur alone or concurrently with an addiction. The best thing, however, is that the following categories are treatable through using CBT.

Major Depression

This type of depression is also called major depressive disorder. This disorder occurs when one feels depressed most of the time for most days of the week. Some of the symptoms associated with this disorder are:

- Weight loss or weight gain
- Being tired often
- Trouble getting sleep
- Thoughts of suicide
- Concentration problems
- Feeling restless or agitated

If one experiences five or more of these symptoms on most days for two weeks or longer, then they have this disorder.

Persistent Depressive Disorder (PDD)

This type of depression usually lasts for two years or even longer. The symptoms associated with disorder include:

- Sleeping too much or too little
- Fatigue
- Low self-esteem

Bipolar Disorder

A person with such a disorder usually experiences mood episodes that range from extremes of high energy with an "up" mood to low periods.

How CBT Helps with Negative Thoughts of Depression

The cognitive behavioral therapy understands that when one has low moods, they tend to have negative thinking. This negative thinking usually brings cases of hopelessness, depression, and can also lead to a change in behavior.

CBT, therefore, works to help with the patterns of behavior that need to be changed. In short, it works to recalibrate the part of the brain that keeps a tight hold on happy thoughts.

Five CBT Techniques to Counteract the Negative Thinking of Depression

There are several techniques that one can follow to help with fighting off negative thoughts. Before starting these steps, one should make sure that they are ready to undertake them and should keep track of themselves. Here are some of the steps:

- **Locate the problem and brainstorm for solutions**

The first step is to discover the cause of the problem. This step requires one to talk with one's inner self. Once the idea of what the problem might be dawns on you, write it down in simple words. Then write down a list of things that one can do to improve the problem.

- **Write self-statements to counteract negative thoughts**

Once the cause of the problem has been discovered, it is now time to identify the negative thoughts that seem to pop up in one's brain every time. Write self-statements to counteract each foul view. These self-statements are statements that are going to stuff up the negative thoughts. One should always recall all their self-statements and repeat them back to themselves every time a negative thought pops up. However, these self-statements should continually be refreshed because they can at times be too routine.

- **Find new opportunities to think positive thoughts**

Michael is a person who always sees the negative part of people before noticing their bright side. These people, more often than not, usually get depressed quickly. To remedy this, they should always change their thinking and think positively. This, for example, in the case of Michael, can be like first noticing and appreciating how neat people are. This type of thinking can be tough to change to. Here are some of the recommended ways that one can adjust to such thinking;

- Set one's phone to remind them to reframe their minds to something positive.

- Pairing up with someone who is working on this same technique. This will make one have positive thoughts, and also get to enjoy them with someone else.

- **Finish each day by visualizing its best parts**

After each day, one can write down the most exciting events of the day and try to remember them. Sharing such moments online can even help one form new associations, and also thinking ways that can prove to be very helpful.

- **Learn to accept disappointment as a normal part of life**

In life, disappointment is bound to come one's way. How one deals or behaves after a disappointing event determines how fast one is going to move forward. Take for example John who just lost a job interview. This is a thing that can happen to anyone. The way he responds to this situation will determine how fast he is going to move forward. If he starts getting the thoughts of "I am a failure", "The world is so unfair to me", or even "I will never succeed in life", then he is moving in the wrong direction. The best way to approach this situation is by allowing himself to be disappointed and remembering that he had no control over the situation. Later, he can write some things he has learnt from the experience and things he can do to remedy it next time.

Conclusion

In conclusion, anger and depression are a duo that can affect one's life negatively if not adequately managed. The best way to handle these two feelings is by undergoing a CBT that will help one learn new ways of thinking, which may help one change how they perceive things in life. This can make one view events in a different way for the better. It is also important to note that one usually does not have control over everything in their lives. Some things are just not in one's hands.

CBT, therefore, teaches one how to deal with such situations before they can get the better of someone.

Chapter 7: Deleting BAD Habits and Creating New POSITIVE Ones

Evaluating your thoughts and ideas as the most relevant step of cognitive behavior therapy (CBT)

Killing Subconscious and Conscious Habits

Having a sense of what CBT entails and how useful your thoughts impact different moods and perceptions, you can now move to the one and the most critical first steps of learning how to identify negative thoughts and energy around you.

Why is it Hard to Stick to Good Habits?

We often fell into harmful habits including:

- Smoking
- Stress and junk eating
- Fighting
- Having a boring career
- Watching TV all day
- Stalking someone

But why? Is it always a struggle to change your unhealthy behaviors? Whenever you get inspired to create a change, you find yourself doing the same thing rather than something more desirable? This is because we usually try to implement changes using the wrong method. In this chapter, I will guide you through how to integrate both real-life experiences and science as a way of changing your unhealthy habits for the rest of your life. If you can change your thoughts, you can change your habits.

Differentiate Between Bad Habits and Addictions

It is easy to ignore harmful practices such as smoking to be a small innocent routine that "sometimes" gets out of hand. However, your friends and relatives view it differently; maybe they perceive it to be a developing hidden addiction that needs urgent action.

Remember, not all habits are breakable; you can only change certain habits when you follow this guide. Habits recognized as addictive will require you involve professional counselling, join a support group, or use this self-help book to solve it if you can by yourself.

Are you an addict? Here is the list of questions to ask yourself:

Do you:

- Have financial troubles as a result of spending almost all your income on the activity?
- Endure withdrawal symptoms whenever you stop the

habit? (anger, frustration, restlessness)

- Have health complications affiliated to the activity?
- Prefer this activity to other enjoyable activities?
- Hide or refuse to acknowledge your behavior from people?
- Allow the activity to interfere with your normal routine?
- Seek binges whenever you are on the habit?
- Save extra supplies for emergencies (hiding cans of beer in your bedroom)
- Have trouble balanced your limits on the activity? For instance, one shot of liquor leads you to binge drink the whole bottle to blackout.
- Engage in the activity to deal with emotional and stress problems?
- Participate in dangerous behavior whenever doing the activity?
- Destroy your interpersonal relationship because of this activity?

Some or all of these symptoms are usually experienced by people who languish on alcoholism, binge eating, drug abuse, and smoking. However, it is recommended to seek a professional physician to examine your possible addiction. Here are a few suggestions on ways to go about it other than self-help:

- Visit a psychologist or behavioral therapist who deals

with habits.

- Be a member of a group like NA (narcotics anonymous) or support group.
- Join a promising weight-loss group that provides long-term life changes rather than fad diets.
- Ask your physician for a different non-addictive way to conquer cravings.

Don't hold back to ask help from others, since some addictions can't be overcome by following a simple checklist. If you think you are experiencing troubles with your addiction, then get assistance.

The Science behind Your Habits

(The 3 Rs of habit change)

This is a simple 3-step loop that every habit follows:

- Reminder (what induces the behavior)
- Routine (the activity itself)
- Reward (an advantage you get from doing the action)

This pattern has been approved again and again by behavioral psychology researchers. Let's see how 3 R's works, in reality, using the case of smoking a cigarette.

- ***Step one:*** You smell a cigarette from a distance (reminder). It initiates the behavior. The smells trigger your mind to smoke.

- ***Step two:*** You smoke (routine). The actual habit. Whenever you detect the smell of a cigarette, you have a habit of smoking one or more.

- ***Step three:*** You get stimulated (reward). The benefit gained after smoking. In this case, the reward was getting relaxed and contented from the cigarette smoking.

- ***Results:*** In the case where the reward is positive, then the pattern returns a positive result which tells the brain, "the next time you smell a cigarette, smoke one."

How Can You Create New Habits and Stick to Them?

Here's how:

Creating new positive and productive habits based on the old ones that will make you happy and distract you from the negative emotions.

Step 1: Use a Prevailing Habit as a Reminder for Your New Ones

Friends will tell you that to initiate a new pattern you require to practice self-control, but some of us would tend to disagree. Trying to remember and getting motivated is not a useful way of using CBT. To be motivated is an off and on feeling, right? Therefore, you can't rely on something that changes (motivation) to create something that you want to be regular (new habit).

For this reason, a reminder is such an essential part in creating a new routine. A definite reminder encourages you to initiate your new habit by concealing your new behavior in something that you are currently doing, instead of depending on getting motivated.

For instance, I created a new habit of praying every day before going to bed. The act of going to bed was something that I already did, and it triggers my new behavior. To prevent myself from having to remember to pray, I placed my Bible on the bedside drawer. Whenever I am off to bed the bible will trigger my new habit of praying. A visible reminder like the Bible links the new practice with the ongoing behavior, therefore making it easier to change.

How to Determine Your Reminder

Sticking with your new habit requires you to set up a system that simplifies your start. However, selecting the right reminder for your new habits is the essential step to making change effortless. The reminder should be unique to your life and new pattern you are creating. The best way to find a great reminder for your new habit is to write two lists. The first list contains the things that you do every day without fail. For example:

- Take a shower
- Brush your teeth
- Dress
- Take breakfast
- Go to work
- Sit down for dinner

- Get into bed

Most of this activity is carried out daily and can act as reminders for new habits. For example, after taking breakfast, you immediately go to work.

In the second list, note down things that occur to you each day:

- Your alarm rings
- You get an email
- Your doorbell rings
- A song ends
- The sun sets

These events, when used effectively, can act as triggers for your new habit. For instance, whenever your alarm rings you wake up for work. In the case where you want to be happier, using the list above you can choose a reminder "taking breakfast" and use it to say one thing that you are anticipating and delighted to do for the rest of the day.

Step 2: Make Your Habits Easy to Start

Earlier in this guide, I mentioned how easy it is to get caught up in the desire to create a massive change in your life. We see a fantastic weight loss transformation and anticipate that we need to lose 20 pounds in the next month.

I've experienced the same, so I get it and understand your enthusiasm. I appreciate that you are willing to make a change for the greater good of your life, and I will do what I can to help you accomplish that transformation. It is critical to remember that permanent change starts with small steps of your daily habits, not once in a lifetime transformations.

If you want to start a new healthier habit, then you need to start small. It is said, "Make it so easy that you can't say no". At first, performance doesn't matter. Alternatively what matters is becoming that person who adheres to their new habit- regardless of how small or irrelevant it seems. You can then develop to the level of performance that you desire when your behavior becomes a habit.

Homework: Decide on a new habit you want to start then ask yourself, "How can I make it so easy to do that I can't say no to it?"

Step 3: Reward Yourself

Negative thoughts, anxiety, and depression make us feel bad about ourselves, but we always thrive to continue doing things that create happiness and joy in our hearts. In the case of sticking to new habits, it is important to reward yourself each time you exercise the new habit.

For example, if I'm working to achieve a fit body, then I will regularly tell myself after a workout, "that was a good workout" or, "nice job; you have shed a few calories today."

You could even go the extra mile if you feel like it and tell yourself, "victory" or," excellent" each time you perform your new habit.

"I have done it myself, and I can attest that it is an incredible way of rewarding oneself."

- Pray before going to bed. "success."

- Eat a balanced diet meal. "excellent."

- Go for a morning jog. "superb."

- Clean my room. "Good work."

If you aren't someone who generally does positive self-talk as a way of rewarding yourself, you can get used to it suddenly. No matter how silly it sounds, research has proven that paying yourself a compliment is a vital component of developing your habit. Reward yourself with some credit and celebrate every small achievement.

Consequently, ascertain that the new developing habits that you are expanding are meaningful to you. It will be tough to reward yourself for something that you are only doing to impress others or you think you will get approval from it. Create new habits that you are interested in and familiar with because it is your life, not your friend's or relative's life. Make sure you spend your time on things that are crucial to you specifically.

Step 4: Establish Your Target Goal

Getting rid of bad habits is similar to setting a goal. However, you can't develop new habits without having a clear outcome in mind and with an exact target date. It is essential to appreciate the process of setting goals, finding obstacles, and then adjusting your behaviors to reach those goals.

For example, you can't just say, "I want to lose a few pounds." Instead, you need to find a gym to sign in and have a personal trainer guide you on what to eat and which exercise to do, and the date you will start this journey.

The following would be an excellent goal: "Starting June 3rd, I will no longer sleep past 7 o'clock. Instead, I will wake up, take a healthy breakfast, go for a morning jog, and afterwards attend my gym routine with my trainer." You notice this result has a deadline with a specific outcome. By 3rd June, you will know if the routine is working or not. That's how simple it is to set a goal that will break your bad habits.

Comparatively, since we are stressing a one-month trial period, I propose you create some array of metrics for the end of 30 days. Upon that stated date, you can choose either to continue with the new habit change.

Conclusion

Indeed, cognitive behavioral therapy is useful in evaluating your thoughts that otherwise influence your perceptions and moods. Your brain needs to be trained to identify the difference between bad habits and good ones. This may take longer and require patience, so set a goal and follow the above steps so that you can achieve a long-term change.

Chapter 8: Goal Setting and Time Management

Goal Setting

What is a goal? A goal is the ultimate thing that you would want to do at the end of the treatment or therapy. Goal setting should be very precise and to the point if it is to help someone. What does this mean? For example, instead of just saying that at the end of the program, you would like to feel "less depressed" or even feel "better", one should ask oneself the things that make them "less depressed" or even those that make them feel happy. These things are what one should set as their goals. Some of these things may include:

- To go out and travel or even visit somewhere.
- To get and enjoy a movie with someone.
- To quietly enjoy a good cup of coffee.

These goals can be very enticing to write and thus one may end up with a lot of goals. This should always be avoided because a lot of goals can be very confusing. One should work with about one to three goals. These goals, however, should be reviewed often because they can become too common.

Setting a Goal

This book is aimed at the self-help of the reader. For any self-help to be effective, one should set some goals. These goals should be SMART. What does SMART mean? These goals should be Specific, Measurable, Achievable, Relevant, and lastly, Time limited.

Here are some tips that may be of help when setting a goal:

- Ask yourself what you want to be able to do.

- Be as specific as you can by stating how often you want to do something.

- Set realistic goals.

- State the problems positively. This is by starting them with "to be able to" instead of "to stop".

- Ask someone you know well and trust to help you.

Why are self-help goals usually important? Self-help goals usually help to guide a person. Not having these goals is like finding directions to a place which you didn't want to go to. Apart from goals, one must also identify their triggers. What are triggers? Triggers are situations that cause anxiety or even low moods. One should fight to eliminate these.

Triggers from Self-help

Here are some tips that may help you with this:

- Identify what triggers your anxiety or low mood.

- Look at your own Hot Cross Bun.
- Identify what needs to change for you to feel better.

Goals from Self-Help

Here are some tips that may help with this:

- What do you hope to gain?
- What do you hope to have achieved?
- What will be different for you?

Remember that the goals must be as SMART as possible.

Common Obstacles That You May Face

While trying to reach these self-help goals, one might come across some challenges. These include;

- Worries about getting things 'right' may lead to people not completing these tasks.
- Being very busy and not prioritizing the content and techniques contained in this book.
- Feeling low or unmotivated may make it seem more difficult to do the work.

What do you think could prevent you from being able to achieve these goals?

What could you do to ensure that these obstacles do not prevent you from achieving your goals and overcoming your problems?

Time Management

What is time management? Time management is the ability to use one's time effectively or productively, especially in the workplace. Time management is a skill that involves prioritizing activities and focusing one's resources on the most important one's while eliminating the time wasters and disruptions. Therefore, time management is a skill that involves intense decision making, either large or small, that changes the shape of one's life.

In life no one usually has control of a day's events. Anything is bound to happen. However, one usually has some control over what they can do. This is the power of time management. Even in the cases of structured times, one is able to choose and prioritize activities that they are going to undertake. It is through the exercise of these choices that one has control over their time.

Planning and organizing are two secrets of time management that one must know. For effective time management, one must plan their time in a way that harmonizes with their unique requirements, inclinations, and interests. The goal of time management is usually to eliminate any time wasters. It is important to note, therefore, that even the saving of five minutes in one's schedule can go a long way towards improving one's life by increasing their productivity.

Time management usually begins with an assessment of one's time usage, followed by coming up with a schedule on how to carry out different activities in respect to the time.

Seven Basic Skills to Improve Your Productivity

1. Get Started

For one to improve their productivity, one has to get started on a particular task. Getting the motivation to start is usually a very hard task. In life, the differences between successful people and the others is that they are willing to perform a task. They are always ready. Therefore, it is important for one to bite their own bullet and get down to the tasks at hand.

Most are the times when it is difficult to find self-motivation. In cases like these, one should work out the obstacles and get rid of them – may it be practical or even psychological obstacles.

2. Make it Part of Your Routine

Routines usually create a reassuring framework for each and every day that tasks will be completed. This therefore reduces the hustle of determining what activities to carry out. So, one should create and allocate tasks with time slots and later let the routine guide you through the day.

3. Do not Say YES, when You Want to Say NO

For one to improve their productivity, confidence and self-esteem are two important things to have. It is sometimes difficult to resist the demands of other people, especially friends. This is especially when one is feeling depressed or has lost sight of the important things.

So, keep in mind that every yes that you say, is usually a no to something else. Therefore, it is important for one to find the other thing that is going to be hindered by a yes and try to consider if you can take away time from it.

4. Distant Elephants

Normally, elephants look very small when far away as opposed to when they are near. Therefore, one should always deal with important tasks and not commit themselves to unimportant activities, no matter how far they are.

5. Break it Down

One should break down tasks into smaller realistic and achievable tasks. Large tasks are usually very overwhelming and can cause depression or even anxiety. On the other hand, smaller tasks are usually less overwhelming and, upon completion of each task, one usually has some sense of satisfaction and achievement that fuels them on to the next task.

6. Beware of Perfectionism

Perfectionism is considered to be a very close companion of procrastination. Therefore, for one to increase their productivity, one should not consider how perfectly a task is done. One should only aim at achieving the target. When one aims at the target only, one may even achieve more than expected.

7. Make a Plan

One should then allocate tasks with some time slots in a routine. A few minutes spent making the routine will save hours which could be otherwise wasted.

Cognitive Behavioral Therapy on Goal

Setting and Time Management

CBT helps one in understanding their body cycles. By working with the body cycles, one can maximize their efficiency which is the ultimate goal of time management. How then does one maximize their efficiency by working with their body cycles? Here is a routine that might come in handy:

Cognitive Tasks 6am-8am.

Cognitive tasks are usually carried out in the morning, when the brain is fresh. These tasks may include problem solving or even calculating. They are usually mental tasks.

Short Term Memory 8am-10am.

These tasks may include the last-minute revision for a test.

Long Term Memory 10am-12pm.

These tasks may include going through and memorizing a speech to be given. These tasks are best performed in the afternoon.

Manual Dexterity 2pm-6pm.

Manual dexterity is the ability of someone to use their hands to perform a difficult action skillfully and with ease. These tasks include physical workouts and keyboarding. These activities are best carried out in the early evenings. This is because muscle coordination is at its peak.

Monitor and Reward Behavior

One should always have the habit of acknowledging what they have already achieved rather than that which has not been accomplished. This is very important because it gives one the motivation to take on other tasks. One should also have the habit of rewarding themselves or even taking a break after achieving a particular task.

Personal Time Management Tool

Time Flies Worksheet

When undergoing the CBT training, one should always have such a worksheet. Here, we can call it a timetable. This worksheet helps you determine where you may have some free time. This is after evaluating all your activities. Then one can see how they can improve their schedule.

Understanding Your Results

As one tries to improve their schedule, one should also consider the effects of their choices on their personal health, and also their well-being. One should not squeeze their schedules in a way that there are no breaks for refreshments or even recreation.

Most people usually just manage around 60 hours of productivity each week. If one's result is above this, then one might need to cut back on either work or school. On the other hand, if one's productivity is below 60 hours, then one should be able to balance the demands of the activities, may it be in school or in the workplace.

Causes of Time Wastage

Here are some reasons that can lead to time wastage in someone's life.

1. **Lack of Proper Planning.**

Some people fail to see the benefit of planning their activities. This is maybe the main reason why they do not achieve a lot of tasks, because there is time being wasted somewhere.

To remedy this, therefore, one should recognize that planning takes time but saves time in the long run.

2. **Lack of Priorities.**

Lack of priorities is usually brought about when one does not have goals in life. Therefore, to remedy this, one must set some goals and objectives which will drive you.

3. **Over-Commitment.**

Over commitment can also lead to time wastage. Over-commitment is usually caused by factors like broad interests and the lack of prioritizing these interests. The solution to this, therefore, is abandoning some interests and then deciding which will come first amongst those that remain.

4. Management by Crisis.

Management crisis is usually caused by unrealistic time estimates. One should therefore allow for adequate time, and also be opportunity-oriented so as to remedy this.

5. Haste.

Haste is usually caused by:

- Impatience with detail or routine matters.
- Lack of planning ahead.
- Attempting too much in too little time.

This problem however can be remedied by distinguishing between urgent and important, taking time to plan, attempting less, or maybe taking time to do it right the first time.

6. Visitors.

Visitors are usually brought about by either enjoyment of socializing or maybe the inability to say no. This therefore can be remedied by saying no, doing it elsewhere, or even saying that you are not available.

7. Indecision.

Indecision is usually caused by lack of confidence in the facts or even fear of the consequence of a mistake. This can be remedied by improving fact finding and validating procedures, accepting that risks are inevitable, and also maybe using mistakes as a learning process.

Chapter 9: Other Ways to Support Psychological Health

Apart from using CBT, there are other ways to support psychological and overall mental health. We all recognize the importance of mental health but the main question here is how do we go about achieving it? Possible conditions that compromise proper mental ability include either being born with the defect or having acquired it in the process due to stress, depression, or substance abuse. In the case of it being a birth defect, this book will not help the patient since that is beyond human control. On the other hand, if you acquired it through one of the mentioned ways or similar ones, then keep on reading and thank you for reading this far.

What is Mental Health?

According to WHO (World Health Organization), health, which includes mental health, involves a state of entire mental, physical, and social well-being, which means it's not just about the absence of a disease or condition.

The same definition applies to proper mental health, which implies it's not just about the presence or absence of mental disorders such as anxiety and depression, or bipolar disorders, amongst others. If one is mentally healthy, then it means they are aware of their own capabilities, can cope with life's normal dramas, and will work effectively in a bid to make a mark on his or her community.

We can therefore say that good mental health is the core to the effectiveness of an individual and the community around him or her.

In the Name of Good Mental Health

CBT has done a great job in making people realize themselves and be able to get back on track. It has been used to treat several conditions (you can refer to the Introduction to see what CBT can be used to address).

On the other hand, mental health involves more than one strategy if we need to make sure that positivity stays in us on a long-term basis. Promoting good mental health involves utilizing strategies and prepared programs that generate an enabling environment that has the right living conditions for people to abide by and be able to maintain healthy conditions.

There is no particular program aimed at mental health, and that is why it will involve more than CBT.

The range of programs available should be thanked by those who have benefited, since one specific measure may not suit your troubled neighbor. They all give us a chance to enjoy the fruits of staying positive by allowing the mind to adjust the way it thinks.

What Determines Your State of Mental Health?

Mental health has a range of factors that influence it, which is the same as physical health. The factors are also interactive, and they include psychological, biological, and social aspects. Research has shown that the evidence is well portrayed in poverty, low or improper education, low income earning, or poor housing and sanitation.

The declining socioeconomic status that has more disadvantages will force individuals to succumb to mental disorders. Those who are more vulnerable involve the less fortunate or disadvantaged and within a community prone to mental disorders. If other additional factors such as insecurity, hopelessness, poor body health, increased risks of violence and rapid social change are also around, that also partially explains why we may be having improper mental health.

Ways that You can use to Promote Overall Psychological Wellbeing

Here are some things to consider as you look forward to reinstating good mental health.

Look for What is Affecting You

Since we aren't the same, it is crucial that you investigate your individual causes of ill mental health. On the other hand, some shared causes may be becoming stressed, or depressed, finding difficulty to cope or quit something, or generally upset.

There are life events that may affect our mental health. They include:

- Being lonely
- Loss of someone close to you
- Illicit relationships
- Financial issues
- Work related problems

NB: loneliness, insomnia stress and inactivity are all forms of negativity when it comes to mental wellbeing.

At times, it is almost impossible to determine why we experience mental disorders. While it is a cause to worry, there are other factors that will lead to such feelings. They maybe happened or occurred in the past.

They may involve the following:

- Neglect, child abuse, or violence
- Homelessness, especially for those who have experienced foster care
- Social discrimination
- Terminal illness in us or in the family
- Loss of a job or unemployment
- Poverty and debt

- Trauma associated with life experiences such as high-level crime, military issues or being involved in major tragedies such as bomb attacks

Regardless of the cause, what you need to remember is that you have a right to feel great and there is a protocol for you to achieve that.

Building Relationships That Can Help You

Getting involved in social groups or having a friend will give you a sense of belonging if it's not yet there. It will help you cope with difficulty if you manage to do the following:

- **Connect with loved ones**: Always keep in touch with your friends and relatives with the convenient method available. You can plan to visit, call them, or leave them messages.

- **Joining social groups:** What do you like to do? Some of us like playing instruments, others drawing, swimming, and the list is endless.

- **Talk about your feelings:** If you have someone that you can trust with your personal issues, it's a good idea to open up to them. It also shows that you are aware of what is happening to you, so explaining it to someone actually helps. At times, it is hard to explain it to our friends, but you can do that to a person who has a similar experience. If you have a chance, please utilize it. There are online groups that one can join to express and try to solve mental matters.

Make Time for Yourself

It can appear selfish to set time for yourself, but it is vital to your overall wellbeing and can help you spring out from mental difficulty.

Mindfulness: Having your presence helps you to realize oneself and be able to manage what we feel. The goal here is to enjoy life again and accept what is around you. We will cover this in detail in the next chapter.

Acquire a new skill: If you learn something that you have been longing for, or will help you later, it gives you the confidence and the joy of achievement. You could sign up for a class or try a new language. Whatever it is, it doesn't have to be big.

Relaxing techniques: Do something that soothes your mind such as having a bath, listening to music, or going for a jog. All these and more will help you cope with stress and mental disorders.

Examine Your Mental Health Status

If you are already aware of your mental condition or difficulty, take the appropriate steps to make sure that you are improving.

- ***Talk about what will help you:*** If there is a strategy that worked on you before, tell the one helping you out. Let those close to you know what can support you better such as listening to your troubles or making you aware of your issues.

- ***Stay alert for warning signs***: If you can be aware of how you feel and are able to spot signs that depict you are unwell, that is much better. Being aware of such signs will help you when it becomes hectic, and it will also form the base guidance to those who are directing and supporting you.

- ***Use a mood diary:*** Just like we track our day activities, we can also record our moods, and we have seen that is possible in the previous chapters. Have a way to record your moods, the negative issues that you think of, and ways to help you stay positive. If you have no idea how to write one, there are online sources to help you with that such as moodscope.com

- ***Upgrade your self-esteem:*** It is one of the major steps in making yourself ready to challenge your mental issues.

Physical Health is Vital to Mental Wellbeing

Look after your body and what you are subjecting it to. Here are a few recommended things:

Eating Healthy

- Invest in a good balanced diet
- Eat regularly so that your energy levels are constant, and the body can regulate sugar levels

- Have fruits and vegetables aplenty
- Avoid alcohol and other drugs that ruin mental ability

Moving It

Engage in exercise to keep the juices flowing, which will also help you get rid of negativity. Some activities include:

- A walk
- Bike riding
- Swimming
- Yoga
- Football
- Martial arts
- Etc.

Have Enough Sleep

- Tiredness brings in more worry and stress. Doctors' orders direct you to sleep 8 hours per day.
- Have a bedtime routine, such as drinking milk or hot water before sleeping. Later, you can read a book or listen to music that helps you sleep.
- Sleep and wake up at the same time every day.

- Do not drink anything caffeinated after lunch.

As we wrap up this chapter, it is important to consider other methods that will help you gain better mental health as you continue with CBT. That way, you will have more tolls to conquer what you need to get rid of.

Chapter 10: Maintaining Mindfulness

What does the term mindfulness mean? Mindfulness is the quality or state of being conscious or aware of something. Mindfulness is a quality that everyone usually has. It is a quality that is always present to us in every moment. One only gets to realize it if you can take time to appreciate it. By practicing mindfulness, one also practices the art of creating space for ourselves and our reactions.

How can Mindfulness Help One in Overcoming their Challenges?

Mindfulness can be of importance in overcoming your challenges in that:

1. Mindfulness Gives One Perspective.

In times of anger, mindfulness can come in handy by giving you the ability to view a particular situation with a different perspective. One is therefore able to take a step back and make a sane decision devoid of any emotional judgment.

2. Mindfulness Leads You to Acceptance.

Many are the times when one wishes they could change a difficult situation they are maybe going through. This, however, is usually not possible. Mindfulness, in such a case, will teach you how to accept the outcome. It will also teach you that you may lack the power to change the circumstance, but you have all the power to change your attitude toward the circumstance.

3. Mindfulness Helps You Process Anger.

Often are the times in life when unfair circumstances are out of our control. This can cause anger which can lead to destruction of a lot of things in one's life. Mindfulness in this case will help one to understand their anger, rather than just express it. It will also teach one to respond to situations rather than just reacting to them.

4. Mindfulness Gives You Clarity.

This clarity is usually as a result of the perspective that mindfulness gives you. This is because when one removes the emotional judgment when dealing with a situation, one is able to have a clear view of what really happened. This, therefore, allows one to make informed and clear decisions on what to do next.

5. Mindfulness Helps You to Take Care of Yourself.

Mindfulness, as you may have noticed, involves meditation. It is this meditation that helps one understand their body's needs. Therefore, when one is faced with a particular situation, one is able to listen and act in accordance to their body's needs, and this leads to a self-care routine.

How Does One Maintain their Mindfulness?

Some people may find the art of mindfulness hard to comprehend. However, it is a very simple art that one can understand and maintain. Here are some tips that may help you maintain your mindfulness:

1. Practice Mindfulness during Routine Activities.

This tip might not seem that important to most people. However, it is one of the most helpful ways. On a daily basis, most people do not really put much concern on the daily routine activities that they undertake. These activities may include bathing, brushing teeth, or even taking breakfast. Bringing awareness, however, to these activities can help one maintain their mindfulness.

For example, one may try and focus on the way they breathe, their sight, or even their sense of smell. This can make one realize how these routine activities are fun.

2. Practice Right when You Wake up.

Practicing mindfulness early in the morning can be of much importance. This is because it sets one's nervous system for the rest of the day, and thus increases the chances of other mindful moments within the day.

If one finds it hard to practice mindfulness just after waking up, one should try it after having their breakfast.

3. Let Your Mind Wander.

Being 'busy' mentally is usually an asset to any human. This is because a human brain and mind are designed in such a way that they keep on roaming around. These beneficial brain changes are usually attributed to the act of noticing that your mind has wandered, and then non-judgmentally bringing it back. This act of noticing is usually the act of mindfulness.

4. Keep it Short.

Mindfulness is an act that should be practiced several times a day rather than just setting aside a lengthy session in a day. This is because the human brain responds better to bursts of mindfulness rather than a single lengthy session.

For example, occasionally in a day, one can tune their body to focus on maybe how their clothes feel on their body in that moment, or even how they breathe at that moment.

5. Practice Mindfulness while You Wait.

Waiting is one of the common things that makes most people frustrated. Being kept at the reception of an office for almost an hour or even being stuck in traffic in not an experience anybody likes to have. Waiting, however, can be of much importance when one sees it as an opportunity to practice mindfulness.

For example, while stuck in traffic, one can focus on maybe how the movement of the cars is happening or even focus on how the shoes feel on their feet.

6. Pick a Prompt to Remind You to be Mindful.

It is usually human nature to forget. It is only normal, therefore, for one to rely on something that reminds them of something. In this case one can choose any routine activity that will help you to be mindful. This activity can be maybe drinking coffee.

7. Learn to Meditate.

Meditation is usually taken to be like the language to mindfulness. Normally, one has first to learn the language before they can speak the language. It is in the same manner that one has first to learn how to meditate in order to cultivate one's mindfulness skills. Meditation helps one tap into mindfulness with ease.

In conclusion, mindfulness is not a luxury in life. It is an art that helps one improve their brain's focus, and thus reduce their stress in life. This in the end leads to a better self.

Killing Procrastination

Are you fond of avoiding or putting off tasks? Does this action dispute with your true values and beliefs? It is high time you step back and ask yourself authentic questions. How responsible are you to accomplish the tasks in the course of time (or not)? If it is not practical to abide with it then ask yourself what else you can pull off to transform your life's situations in order to avoid executing the same task later.

Do you still find yourself procrastinating certain work that is harmonious with your real values and is essential to achieve your goals? These are the task that requires your energy and positive attitude of learning how to finish it more efficiently and within the deadline. Here is a guide on how you can accomplish your task in your best interest without procrastinating.

1. Stop Worrying

If you take a pause you will notice that we spend most of our time worrying about what is required of us to do instead of focusing our time on actually performing the task that needs to be done. Considerably, it is possible that if we redirected time wasted on worrying and thinking about the task and invest it in more useful manner, you will realize you are almost finishing your task(s).

Usually, this is easier said than done. Firstly, start this process by use of consciousness to acknowledge the times in any given moment when you discover yourself full of worry and rumination. When you discover this, use this incident as a chance to remind yourself to convert your energy in a proper creative manner.

2. Start Small

Once you start working on your task you actually realize it is less demanding than they appear to be. When you are faced with huge workloads or obstacles you can decide to break down tasks into smaller categories and assigning a deadline for each task group. This is an effective and efficient way to carry out your tasks in order to accomplish them on time.

If your desk is stuck with a pile of papers and reports, it is easy to glimpse at it and become overpowered by its absolute weight. Preferably, look at the pile of papers for literally what it is (one simple sheet of paper on top of another sheet). By doing this you will be able to take things to step by step, and at the end you realize you have accomplished a great deal within a short time.

3. Save the Cost of Wasting Time

Do you know the more time you waste on avoiding something uninteresting, troublesome, and repulsive, the more it will cost you later to perform the same task? No matter how much you evade a task it rarely vanishes on its own. It will calmly wait for you to work on it, and during the procrastination period, it is possible that it has piled up into some vulgar appendage for you pull off.

Let's take this example: take out a clean sheet of paper and subdivide it into two columns. Under the first column write down a list of all the irresistible reasons to perform the task (rewards and benefits). Under the second column make a list of all possible reasons to not to do the work (they are the benefits you believe to achieve by avoiding the task). Have a look at the two columns. Which do you see is longer and more reasonable? It is likely that the most effective choice is to take care of the task now rather than later.

4. Challenge Negative Beliefs

It is a common thing for cognitive distortions to get in the way and obstruct the completion of unsatisfactory tasks within the deadline. Start by discovering and observing your own thoughts with better care and clarity. Do you notice what messages you might be sending yourself via a habitual loop of thinking?

Using CBT, begin to rethink your thoughts and identify negative thoughts. Consider them merely for what they are (just thoughts). Thoughts are just created words and pictures that run through your mind. They will bear meaning if you assign them one. Challenge your ridiculous and negative values and question the soundness of your thoughts with absolute apprehensive knowledge. The moment you start thinking positively you reap more benefits.

5. Search for Hidden Rewards

Identify the expected rewards and benefits you will achieve upon accomplishing (and not finishing) the undesirable task that you may have left without notice. What is the short-term and permanently secondary gains that you can anticipate after completing or not completing the task? For instance, a few people procrastinate due to subliminal fear of failure, or because they are such perfectionists. On the other hand, consider how deciding to finish the task will adversely result in reducing anxiety and stress.

Obstacles to Mindfulness and How to Conquer Them

Our current life presents itself daily with different challenges which are not easy, but at times it is highly rewarding. The best way to move forward from one point to the next is to understand the possible troubles and problems and plan a strategy in advance on how you will overcome them. The following ways show how you can overcome your mindfulness obstacles.

1. Mindfulness is a Continuous Effort

Mindfulness takes a lot of effort, but the longer you are persistent the simpler it gets and the more appreciating your life turns. At the very beginning, your thoughts are full of confusion and every little thing seems more challenging. Being in that situation you end up feeling defenseless and trapped, yet when you focus your attention on being who you really are, the easier it becomes to achieve a peaceful mind.

Throughout your day it is important to practice mindfulness. Don't just wait until you sit down so that you can meditate. Concentrate on being aware of your thoughts when you are carrying out your daily routine and it will be obvious to stay mindful when stuff gets tough.

2. Be Aware of Distractions

The journey of becoming mindful is not a smooth road. It appears to be as if the world is throwing problems at you just to challenge your mind. The distractions could be anything from your daily problems, relationship drama, or negative beliefs.

It is best to practice self and mind awareness when you are still young. The more you conquer these obstacles you become better, stronger, and more aware of yourself. Your friends, teachers, and parents are a few people that are supposed to help you discover who you truly are.

3. Progress Takes Time

Progress may appear to be extremely slow. Several times you may find yourself stuck to situations and stuff that you are interested in, which later may not be present. It is unthinkable to be mindful when you are engrossed in the future or still stuck in the past.

Admittedly we all find ourselves in that situation. The more you want something, the more you are obsessing on not having it and desire to have it. Once you start appreciating and become grateful for what you have now, you will realize your life drifting.

4. The Urge to Give up

Like any other journey, the urge to give up may pursue you now and then. During this time, you will be frustrated and almost give up. The world presents itself with similar seasons of cold, heat, and longer winters which come and go. The same thing applies to our life, and when you notice that, the challenging times are there to provide guidance and help you grow, and you will eventually feel relaxed and peaceful.

5. Don't Forget that the Journey is the Destination

Have ever realized upon reaching a destination it is not as breathtaking as you thought it would be? Most people forget the fact that the reward of a journey is the journey itself. It is a great joy to accomplish your goals, but it will be devastating if you don't replace that goal with another one. Human beings are dreamers and we all work towards achieving certain goals in our life. People around the world need goals so that they can have a sense of purpose and achievement. It is through the journey that we learn, grow, and transform into a better person. Whenever you exercise mindfulness remember there isn't a final destination, and rather focus on the current happenings and the rest will sort itself.

6. Don't Run from Your Problems

Will you be surprised to notice, no matter how enlightened on earth you are, you will still face difficult times and confusing thoughts? The difference is how you are willing to accept the moments for what they really are. When you are able to accept the difficult situation, you will be the protector of your inner space, and it is the only way to guarantee peace of mind.

7. Your Goals may Question Your Mindfulness

Setting goals is desirable and efficient for your journey, but when you become attached to them, something undesirable happens. When you are too invested in achieving your goal, you will start feeling frustrated, pissed, and negative.

Attachment disorients our clarity. Many times, you are working towards your goals with the hope of achieving happiness. Do not allow your goals to pull you into a stressful state of mind. If you concentrate on the good things around you, you will gain more happiness in the long term and right now.

Chapter 11: Homework

This is the last but most important chapter of all. On the other hand, you cannot work on this chapter if you don't have an understanding of the above information. Here, there is some homework for you during the week.

This is an essential component in your self-help therapy, since you will be using what you have already learnt in the previous chapters to fill in your thoughts, feelings, and behaviors before developing steps on how to challenge, cope, and arrive at new strategies.

You will be able to acquire and practice new skills before restructuring the negative beliefs and thinking modes. One may lead you to believe that attending therapy sessions is more important than the homework given. What you need to know is that, even when attending sessions, how you will handle the work given to you is dependent on the effectiveness of the sessions.

If we don't use homework to record our thoughts, insights and plans, then we are at risk of allowing the negative behavior and thoughts to override the opportunity of constructing a new positive way of doing things.

Below, we will help you to attend to the following:

- Capturing negative thoughts
- Recording cognitive distortions
- Dealing with anxiety and stress

- Dealing with anger and depression
- Setting your goals
- Practicing mindfulness

Are you ready? Here is an assignment to go through during the week. Depending on your problem above, fill in on what you need to address.

Capturing Negative Thoughts (NATs)

In a bid to reconstruct your thinking pattern, here is a worksheet for you to fill in when you are ready to capture the negative thoughts. Once you have practiced how to capture negative thoughts in chapter 4, use the information to fill in below.

Situation	NATs	Emotions	Challenging the thought	The balanced thought	Revisit your emotions
Remember the troubling situation	What negative thought came into your mind as the first reaction?	What did you feel? Describe it with one word and rate it with a scale of 0-100%	What is the counter thought that is based on factual evidence and challenges the NATs?	What was the balancing thought after challenging the NATs?	How are your previous emotions now? Rate them 0-100%
Situation 1:					

Situation 2:					

Working on Cognitive Distortions

In chapter 4, we talked about trapping your thoughts. Here is a table to fill in for that. Tick the cognitive distortions that you have been going through and then record how they have been affecting your life against the ticked ones.

If you still do not remember what the words in the cognitive distortion column mean to you, revisit the trapping thoughts section in chapter 4 for more information before filling in the table.

Cognitive distortion	Tick against the one affecting you	Write how the ticked one has affected your life
All or nothing thinking		

Labelling		
Focusing on negativity or filtering your thoughts		
Use of 'should' and 'must' in your to-do statements		
Blame game		
Foretelling		
Overgeneralization		
Mind reading		
Emotional reasoning		
Catastrophizing		
Personalizing		
Jumping to conclusions		

Challenging the Cognitive Distortions

Here, after recording the distortions above, the next table is to help you challenge them. There is an example below each cell to help you in filling it out.

Situation	What did you think?	Cognitive distortion	Emotion	Supporting your emotions	Challenging your thoughts
I did not finish my assignment.	The assignment was too hard. I never found time to do it.	Focusing on the negative.	Stressed, frustrated	I'm a useless person who cannot plan anything or stick to their plan. I simply cannot remember such during the weekend with a party at hand.	I never found time to study. I went to my friend's birthday on the weekend that I was supposed to do it. I need to find time to recover. otherwise it will be too bad.

Dealing with Anxiety and Stress

Here is a table that will help you record your source of stress or anxiety and the alternative thought to challenge the source of the bad thought. It is important that you use logic in reasoning to come up with what happened in the event and what you know to counter the situation.

Stressing/anxious situation or thought	Challenging the thought
Record the anxious thought	Has the anxious thought come into reality at any time in your life?
What made the thought come up in the first place?	If it did happen, what would be the outcome?
How often do I feel this way?	Is there a situation that is most likely going to disprove what you are thinking?

What situation validates the anxiety or stress?	If it happens, what will go on? Is it the worst-case scenario you could be expecting?
Any worst-case scenario about your current feeling?	What do you need to remember about the event that will help you to cool down?

Dealing with Anger and Depression

Do you remember the negative thinking table? Use it to counter depression and angry negative thoughts below.

What are you depressed about? Remember, what is making you angry or depressed?	NATs What negative thought came into your mind?	Emotions What did you feel? Describe it with one word and rate it with a scale of 0-100%	Challenging the thought What is the counter thought that is based on factual evidence and challenges the NATs?	The balanced thought What was the balancing thought after challenging the depression thought?	Revisit your emotions How are your previous emotions now? Rate them 0-100%
Situation 1:					

Situation 2:					

Lastly, here is a table for you to record what you are grateful about every day.

Days	**What you are grateful for**
Monday	
Tuesday	
Wednesday	

Thursday	
Friday	
Saturday	
Sunday	

Exercise on Goals Setting

Below, record what puts you in a low mood.

What makes me feel low:

Goals after self-help

Remember the SMART model as you answer the following:

- What do you want to gain?
- What do you need to achieve?
- What will be different after attaining your goals?

My goals:

Record the Obstacles

Here, record what you think could prevent you from achieving the set objectives.

What can prevent me from attaining my goals?

Make sure that you overcome the obstacles.

What will I do to make sure that I achieve my objectives?

Practicing Mindfulness

When dealing with your difficulty, it is a good idea to have something that can help you relieve and re-position yourself. Since we tend to get carried away by our thoughts and things to do, having some mindful techniques ready whenever you feel stressed will make sure that you are always a stride ahead of your troubling thoughts, feelings, and behavior.

Here are some mindful meditation tasks that you can utilize next time you feel like it's too much.

Meditation while Walking

- Take a route for a walk. While walking, notice what is around you – the buildings, plants, people, and the accompanying smell. As for the smell, don't go to a route where the smell does not motivate you.

- As you walk, resist the negative thoughts that are bound to take your sensibility away, since you need your senses at the point of walking. Use this time to focus on what is currently happening. Since you are walking, there is nothing to do to settle anything, so you are helping yourself by staying away for a while.

Body Scanning

It is a technique that helps you to come to your senses whenever you feel overwhelmed by thoughts or feelings from a particular situation. Here is how you go about it:

1. Find a quiet place to sit and close your eyes.
2. Start contemplating your body, note your posture position. Where are your hands and feet?
3. Start moving your fingers and toes in a flaring motion. Feel how they all flow and note the stretch they are making on your hands and feet.
4. Now, it's time to roll your head, clockwise three times. As you do it, make sure you are feeling the weight of your head. Were you doing it clockwise? Now do the same in an anticlockwise direction.
5. Next, imagine an electrical impulse travelling in your body. Begin from your toes all the way up to your knees, the hips, your spine, shoulders, before getting to your head. Once it gets on your head, imagine it trickling down in the same manner to your toes where it all began. Repeat one or two more times.
6. Repeat steps 4, 3 and 2 in that order.

7. Once you are done, open your eyes. What's your feeling now?

Object Meditation

Are you a logical or concrete person? It is essential that you utilize what will juice up the senses as you meditate. Use the following in a bid to reposition yourself:

- ***Auditory aid:*** Some soothing music, tracks with some natural sounds, or white noise.

- ***Visual aid:*** A moving light that is also changing. It could also include a soothing painting, or just staring at a blank wall.

- ***Tangible aid:*** A fidget spinner, rubber bands, or yarn.

- ***Scented aid:*** Cooking, scented candles, fragrances, etc.

At the end of your homework, always remember to work on what you have resolved to do to solve what is troubling your mind. Remember, that is where it all starts.

Conclusion

We all want and need to live a happier life which does not come easy. Before we end the CBT self-help therapy, the question is, how do you condition yourself to live through a complex life with drama all around it?

A sober frame of mind to tackle your feelings and behavior.

At the end of this therapy, you will note many things about yourself, things that you never thought would cross your mind. Remember that you will be judging yourself so that you can scrutinize your problem from all angles and adjust it through changing your thoughts, which in turn changes your feelings and how you behave.

As you learn how to cope with your difficulties, you will be revisiting this book less often since the methods will have stuck from the practice that you have gone through. It is important to understand the importance of practice. The moment you do it for the first two months, you will have captured a wide scope of the problem, plus other related issues that come along. So, whenever negative thoughts pop up, you will be able to counter them using the CBT techniques, and any other useful tools that we have mentioned when maintaining your psychological well-being.

Once you have resolved your problems, it is crucial that you keep the techniques with you until you have fully mastered the art of coping with your issues the right way instead of using negative thoughts. If you are now recovering and moving forward to stay happier, use an exit process that does not make you stop abruptly.

After walking yourself through the steps and techniques, write down a summary of what you have learnt about yourself and your thoughts. It could be on the back of a card that you can put in your wallet. For example, if you learnt how to capture and counter your thoughts, then you have understood that thoughts are not facts and we can choose how to think and react to situations. That is a lesson that you can jot down.

After that you can associate your lesson with the techniques that you came up with to cope with your difficulty. For example, in countering a negative though brought about by stress, you can choose to resolve the stress by walking or listening to soothing music and sounds. That means you have an action plan that you develop to cope with the problem in future when it occurs.

Concerns to Address at the End of Reading

1. Being Able to Cope on Your Own

You are your own boss in this self-help therapy. That means you should be able to cope with the issues affecting your life and overall functionality by practicing the homework assigned. That way, you will allow yourself to always come up with self-talk that enables you to clearly outline the problem and devise the method to make you better and approach the situation with a mind based on factual evidence and a working action plan. Since the lessons are sticking in your head, you should be looking to solve the problems without any help at all, apart from what you have learnt from this therapy.

2. Sorting Out all Your Problems

CBT will not solve all your mental and behavioral problems. On the other hand, it will solve what is listed in the introduction section, and you have the ability to use the skills in the future to work on other issues. Therefore, you should see yourself as a human being who is equipped with life skills to tackle problems when they come.

3. Curing Yourself

Using CBT is not intended to cure the occurrence of negative thoughts or your problem forever. According to Beck, the founder of Cognitive Behavioral Therapy, you need to use the cognitive skills to manage the situation more effectively. When you are managing yourself, the skills become more effective in tackling problematic issues and learning from the tackle for future cases.

4. Addressing the Real Problem

At times, we find ourselves not talking about what is really affecting us. This book is meant for such situations. If you know you are addressing a problem that you are not feeling free to communicate to your friends or therapist, it is possible to view it and solve it on your own with the steps provided. At the end of the day, it is better when we face the real situation instead of beating around the bush and using the skills to solve something unrelated to you.

5. *Looking Forward to a Happier Life*

When therapy is over, and you are feeling alright, at times, you can be faced with the worry that you won't be able to handle yourself outside therapy. You can refer this to as 'falling out' which happens after therapy sessions. Always remind yourself that what you are thinking is not true and you can revisit how to capture negative thoughts and challenge them.

Do you see how CBT techniques can even help you solve how you will be tackling your problems? You also need to note that it is a common problem that many of us face, and working on it is better than submitting to the fear of relapse.

Maintain Your Gains at all Times

Before we conclude, it is essential to address the reason why you need to maintain your achievements. Achieving the gains is easy but we cannot say the same about maintaining them. It is common to think that once you have acquired what you are looking for, the benefits will stick in you magically and forever. From experience, thinking that way will make you fall back on what you solved sooner than you thought.

Therefore, the question you should ask yourself is this: how do you intend to keep the progress that you have developed so far? How many sessions do you need or how many times do you need to revisit the techniques offered in order to guarantee the longevity of what you have learnt?

Have a message that helps you stick to your values, such as 'Use it to live happier and less worried.' Such messages will help you every time you need to troubleshoot future events.

Conclusion

Congratulations on finishing Cognitive Behavioural Therapy, by now you should have a strong understanding towards how you can turn your negative thoughts into positive ones. Enjoy being more confident in yourself, handling future situations the right way and ultimately living a much happier life.

I wish you luck on your journey to health and happiness!

If you found this book helpful please leave a positive review on Amazon as it is greatly appreciated and keeps me being able to deliver high quality books.

CPSIA information can be obtained
at www.ICGtesting.com
Printed in the USA
BVHW061204130519
548121BV00014B/778/P